SUSAN ALTMAN

EXTRAORDINARY
AFRICAN-AMERICANS

REVISED EDITION

CHILDREN'S PRESS®
A Division of Scholastic Inc.
New York · Toronto · London · Auckland · Sydney
Mexico City · New Delhi · Hong Kong
Danbury, Connecticut

This book is dedicated to my parents, Sophie and Norman Altman, who tried to instill in their children a sense of justice, an appreciation of freedom, and a respect for the rights of others.

It is further dedicated to the memory of Addie Mae Collins, Denise McNair, Carole Robertson, Cynthia Wesley, Emmett Till, and Godfrey Sicelo Dlomo, six young people whom freedom failed to reach and justice failed to protect.

Interior design by Elizabeth Helmetsie

Library of Congress Cataloging-in-Publication Data

Altman, Susan.
      Extraordinary African-Americans : from colonial to contemporary times / by Susan Altman.—2nd ed.
        p. cm.—(Extraordinary people)
      Rev. ed. Of: Extraordinary Black Americans from colonial to contemporary times. 1989.
      Includes bibliographical references and index.
      ISBN 0-516-22549-9 (lib. bdg.)   0-516-25962-8 (pbk.)
      1. African Americans—Biography—Juvenile literature. [1. African Americans—Biography.] I. Altman, Susan. Extraordinary Black Americans from colonial to contemporary times. II. Title. III. Series.

E185.96 .A56 2001
920'.009296073—dc21

00-052373

CHILDREN'S PRESS

Contents

12 Foreword

13 Preface

15 List of Abbreviations

16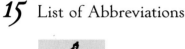
Lucy Terry Prince
Poet
1733–1821

18
Jean Baptiste Pointe DuSable
Frontier Trader,
Founder of Chicago
1745–1818

20
Crispus Attucks
Sailor, Patriot
1723–1770

22
Benjamin Banneker
Inventor, Mathematician,
Astronomer, Surveyor
1731–1806

24
Phillis Wheatley
Poet
1753–1784

26
Peter Salem
Revolutionary War Soldier
1750–1816

28
James Armistead
Revolutionary War Spy
1760–1832

30
Elizabeth Freeman
Abolitionist
1742–1829

32
Richard Allen
Religious Leader,
Abolitionist
1760–1831

34
Gabriel Prosser
Slave Rebellion Leader
1776–1800

36
York
Explorer, Scout, Interpreter
1770–1832

38
Denmark Vesey
Slave Rebellion Leader
1767–1822

40

Black Seminoles

51

The Underground Railroad

61

Jermain Wesley Loguen
Abolitionist, Minister,
Underground Railroad Conductor
1813–1872

43

Nat Turner
Slave Rebellion Leader
1800–1831

54

Lewis Temple
Inventor
1800–1854

63

Frederick Douglass
Abolitionist, Newspaper
Editor, Orator
1817–1895

45

**Joseph Cinque
(Sengbe Pieh)**
Leader of Slave Ship Uprising
1817–1879

55

Dred Scott
Plaintiff in Slave Lawsuit
1795–1858

66

Sojourner Truth
Abolitionist, Women's
Rights Activist, Preacher
1797–1883

48

James Pierson Beckwourth
Frontiersman, Scout, Explorer
1798–1866

57

Lewis Hayden
Abolitionist, State Legislator
1815–1889

68

Robert Smalls
Civil War Hero, Congressman
1839–1915

50

Norbert Rillieux
Inventor
1806–1894

59

Harriet Ross Tubman
Underground Railroad
Conductor, Abolitionist
1821–1913

70

**The Emancipation
Proclamation**
1863

72

African-American Civil War Soldiers
1861–1865

85

Jan Ernst Matzeliger
Inventor
1852–1889

95

George Washington Carver
Scientist, Educator
1861–1943

76

Reconstruction
1865–1877

87

Isaac Myers
Labor Leader
1835–1891

98

Granville T. Woods
Inventor
1856–1910

78

P. B. S. Pinchback
Congressman
1837–1921

89

George Jordan
Soldier
1847–1904

100

Daniel Hale Williams
Surgeon, Educator
1858–1931

80

Booker T. Washington
Educator, Presidential Advisor
1856–1915

91

Scott Joplin
Composer, Pianist
1868–1917

102

Madam C. J. Walker
Businesswoman, Humanitarian
1867–1919

83

Nat Love
Cowboy
1854–1921

93

George Washington Williams
Historian, Lawyer, Soldier
1849–1891

104

Charles Young
Soldier
1864–1922

106

Elijah McCoy
Inventor
1843–1929

117

Mary McLeod Bethune
Educator, Civil Rights Activist
1875–1955

128

Henry Johnson
World War I Hero
1897–1929

107

Henry Ossawa Tanner
Artist
1859–1937

119

W. E. B. Du Bois
Civil Rights Leader,
Anthropologist, Educator
1868–1963

130

Bessie Smith
Blues Singer
1894–1937

109

Ida. B. Wells-Barnett
Journalist,
Civil Rights Activist
1862–1931

122

Robert Sengstacke Abbott
Newspaper Publisher,
Civil Rights Activist
1870–1940

132

**The Great
Northern Migration**

112

Mary Church Terrell
Civil Rights Activist, Educator
1863–1954

124

Garrett Augustus Morgan
Inventor
1875–1963

134

James Weldon Johnson
Writer, Songwriter, Civil
Rights Leader, Diplomat
1871–1938

114

Matthew Alexander Henson
Explorer
1866–1955

126

William Christopher Handy
Musician, Composer
1873–1958

136

Elizabeth "Bessie" Coleman
Pilot
1896–1926

138

Marcus Garvey
Black Nationalist
1887–1940

149

Alain Leroy Locke
Philosopher, Educator, Writer
1885–1954

160

Billie Holiday *(1915–1959)*
Ella Fitzgerald *(1918–1996)*
Jazz Singers

140

**Harlem
Renaissance**
Approx. 1919–1930

151

Carter G. Woodson
Historian
1875–1950

162

Richard Wright
Writer
1908–1960

142

Louis Armstrong
Jazz Musician
1901–1971

153

**Edward Kennedy
"Duke" Ellington**
Musician, Composer, Bandleader
1899–1974

165

Julian Francis Abele
(1881–1950)
Paul Revere Williams
(1894–1980)
Architects

144

Zora Neale Hurston
Writer, Anthropologist
1901–1960

155

Charles Hamilton Houston
Law Professor
1895–1950

167

Paul Robeson
Actor, Singer, Political Activist
1898–1976

146

Langston Hughes
Writer
1902–1967

157

Jesse Owens
Olympic Track
and Field Athlete
1913–1980

169

Joe Louis
Heavyweight Boxing Champion
1914–1981

171

Marian Anderson
Opera Singer
1897–1993

174

**Leroy Robert
"Satchel" Paige**
Baseball Pitcher
1906–1982

176

Asa Philip Randolph
Union Organizer,
Civil Rights Leader
1889–1979

178

Charles Richard Drew
Physician, Scientist
1904–1950

181

Jackie Robinson
Baseball Player
1919–1972

184

Gordon Parks
Photographer, Movie
Director, Writer
1912–

186

Percy Lavon Julian
Chemist
1899–1975

188

Ralph Bunche
Diplomat
1903–1971

190

Miles Davis, Jazz Musician,
Trumpeter *(1926–1991)*
John Coltrane, Jazz Musician,
Saxophonist *(1926–1967)*

192

Lorraine Hansberry
Playwright
1930–1965

194

James Baldwin
Writer
1924–1987

197

Wilma Rudolph
Olympic Track
and Field Athlete
1940–1994

199

Rosa Parks
Civil Rights Activist
1913–

202

Alex Palmer Haley
Writer
1921–1992

204

Ella Josephine Baker
Civil Rights Activist
1903–1986

206

Thurgood Marshall
Supreme Court Justice
1908–1993

218

Fannie Lou Hamer
Civil Rights Leader
1917–1977

229

Martin Luther King, Jr.
Civil Rights Leader
1929–1968

209

**The Little
Rock Nine**

220

Malcolm X
Black Power Leader
1925–1965

234

**The Black
Power Movement**

211

Medgar Evers
Civil Rights Leader
1925–1963

223

**The 1963 March
on Washington**

237

Marian Wright Edelman
Children's Advocate
1939–

213

Sit-Ins

225

Roy Wilkins
Civil Rights Leader
1901–1981

239

Maya Angelou
Poet, Writer
1928–

215

Freedom Riders

227

Alvin Ailey *(1931–1989)*
Arthur Mitchell *(1934–)*
Dancers, Choreographers

241

Guion Stewart Bluford, Jr.
(1942–)
Mae C. Jemison *(1956–)*
Astronauts

244

Muhammad Ali
Heavyweight Boxing
Champion
1942—

255

Colin Luther Powell
Secretary of State, General
1937—

265

Michael Jeffrey Jordan
Basketball Player
1963—

246

Toni Morrison
Novelist, Editor
1931—

257

Alice Walker
Writer
1944—

267

Benjamin S. Carson
Pediatric Neurosurgeon
1951—

248

Jesse Jackson
Minister, Civil Rights Leader
1941—

259

Arthur Robert Ashe, Jr.
Tennis Player
1943—1993

269

**Shelton Jackson
"Spike" Lee**
Movie Director, Producer
1957—

251

John Robert Lewis
Civil Rights Leader,
U.S. Congressman
1940—

261

Henry Louis "Hank" Aaron
Baseball Player
1934—

271

Tiger Woods
Golfer
1975—

253

Bill Cosby
Comedian, Author,
Philanthropist
1937—

263

Oprah Winfrey
Television Talk Show Host,
Actress, Movie Producer
1954—

273 Elizabeth Eckford's Account
of Day One at Central High School

276 Organizations and Online Sites

277 For Further Reading

278 Index

287 Photo Credits

288 About the Author

Foreword

Human beings are not born extraordinary. Nor are they born with courage, or patience, or willpower. These are traits that very ordinary people develop over time. People who see a wrong and decide to right it regardless of how long or how hard they have to work; people who refuse to let go of an idea or a dream even when others call them foolish; people who spend endless days and nights developing a God-given talent; and people who risk their lives, even die, for basic human dignity: these are extraordinary people. They are not born that way, they become that way.

Keep this in mind as you read the biographies of the African-Americans in this book. Each was confronted with a difficult, if not terrible, situation. Each found a way to overcome and triumph. Here you will read about ordinary people who refused to be dehumanized by slavery and discrimination and, instead, fought for freedom and equality with all their might. Some fought in wars to keep America free, some founded and built America's cities, some were great scientists, and some were great leaders. Few were expected to accomplish all that they did, but they all found a way to overcome prejudice based on the color of their skin.

Americans owe a great debt to these people and others like them. They epitomize everything this nation stands for. They took advantage of the principles of democracy and insisted on being free and equal to all men and women. They made a way out of no way. They demonstrated the highest level of citizenship with the strength and brilliance of a determined people.

Deborah Gray White, Professor and Chair
Rutgers University History Department, New Brunswick, NJ
Spring 2001

Preface

America is home to people of almost every race, religion, and nationality. Some, like the Native Americans and Inuit, have been here for thousands of years. Others, who arrived later, came in the hope of finding riches, adventure, and a new life. And some, fleeing war, famine, and persecution, sought only safety and a chance to survive. African-Americans alone were brought here unwillingly, stolen from their homes and forced to live as slaves.

Yet, in spite of this cruel beginning, African-Americans have played a major role in defining and shaping American beliefs, traditions, and customs. From the beginning, they have helped ensure the nation's security and economic well-being. They are among our earliest explorers and have been among the first people to expand and settle the frontier.

Of the people profiled in these pages, many were selected because of the contributions they made to our life and culture. Others were chosen because of the part they played at critical points in our history. Some are presented because they allow readers to better explore the African-American presence in areas where it has often been ignored.

This book represents a small fraction of the thousands of African-Americans who have added to the growth and development of this country. Of those not mentioned, some are well known, and their lives and work are covered extensively elsewhere. Many more remain anonymous. In some cases, the record of their accomplishments has been left to fade under the glare of onrushing events. In other cases, no record existed in the first place.

Many of the men and women in this book overcame incredible hardships with little to sustain them but their own courage and determination.

How many others tried but were crushed under the wheels of unremitting repression will never be known. But some did survive. Some did triumph.

Like other racial, religious, and ethnic groups, African-Americans have made their presence felt in fields ranging from science and industry to literature, education, religion, and the arts. Yet, it may be that the main contribution of African-Americans has not been in any specific area but rather to democracy itself. For in the struggle to secure, protect, and defend their own rights, they have helped guarantee the rights of everyone else.

Susan Altman
Washington, D.C.

List of Abbreviations

AME	African Methodist Episcopal Church
ASNLH	Association for the Study of Negro Life and History
CORE	Congress of Racial Equality
DAR	Daughters of the American Revolution
MFDP	Mississippi Freedom Democratic Party
MIA	Montgomery Improvement Association
NAACP	National Association for the Advancement of Colored People
NACW	National Association of Colored Women
NASA	National Aeronautics and Space Administration
NYA	National Youth Administration
OAAU	Organization of Afro-American Unity
OCS	Officers' Candidate School
PUSH	People United to Serve Humanity
SCLC	Southern Christian Leadership Conference
SNCC	Student Nonviolent Coordinating Committee
UCLA	University of California, Los Angeles
UN	United Nations
UNIA	Universal Negro Improvement Association

Lucy Terry Prince

Poet

1733–1821

The Bar's Fight ·-•-

August 'twas the twenty-fifth
Seventeen hundred forty-six
The Indians did in ambush lay
Some very valiant men to slay
'Twas nigh unto Sam Dickinson's mill
The Indians there five men did kill
The names of whom I'll not leave out
Samuel Allen like a hero fout
And though he was so brave and bold
His face no more shall we behold
Eleazer Hawks was killed outright
Before he had time to fight
Before he did the Indians see
Was shot and killed immediately
Oliver Amsden he was slain

Which caused his friends much grief
    and pain
Simeon Amsden they found dead
Not many rods off from his head.
Adonijah Gillet, we do hear
Did lose his life which was so dear
John Saddler fled across the water
And so escaped the dreadful slaughter
Eunice Allen see the Indians coming
And hoped to save herself by running
And had not her petticoats stopt her
The awful creatures had not cotched her,
And tommyhawked her on the head
And left her on the ground for dead.
Young Samuel Allen, Oh! lack-a-day
Was taken and carried to Canada

·-•-

This poem describes a Native American attack on Deerfield, Massachusetts, a small settlement on the western border of the Massachusetts Bay Colony. Written by Lucy Terry, a sixteen-year-old slave girl, the poem is considered to be the best description of the account on record.

The attack occurred in 1746, not long before the French and Indian War (1754–63). Although Terry's poem describing the massacre was not published until 1855, it was a favorite in colonial New England. It was read often at town meetings and on various social occasions.

The events Terry describes in her poem are not too far from some of those in her own life. She was kidnapped from her home in Africa when she was only five and sold to a family in Deerfield, where she grew up. There she met and married Abijah Prince, an ex-slave who had gained his freedom after serving in the French and Indian War.

Shortly after they were married, Abijah Prince purchased Lucy's freedom in 1756, and the two of them moved to a farm in Guilford, Vermont. Eventually, they had six children, two of whom fought in the Revolutionary War (1775–83). Abijah Prince also became one of the fifty-five original founders of the town of Sunderland in Vermont.

Two years after the Revolution, a wealthy neighbor tried to force the Princes off their land. Abijah was then almost eighty years old, so Lucy, twenty-five years younger than her husband, rode across Vermont to seek the aid of the governor's council. Fortunately, the council sided with the Princes and ordered the neighbor to leave them alone.

In 1794, Abijah died. For the next eighteen years, Lucy rode horseback over the mountains to visit his grave. When yet another neighbor tried to claim her property, she fought back, this time taking her case all the way to the Vermont Supreme Court. After ruling in her favor, the judge told her that she had made one of the most convincing arguments he had ever heard.

Lucy Terry Prince, America's first poet of African descent, died in 1821 at the age of eighty-eight. The remarkable sixteen-year-old girl who had written "The Bar's Fight" turned out to be a courageous fighter herself.

Jean Baptiste Pointe DuSable

Frontier Trader, Founder of Chicago
1745–1818

Chicago is the third largest urban center in the United States. It was an African-American man named Jean Baptiste Pointe DuSable who first put the city on the map.

It is generally believed that DuSable was born in Saint Domingue (now Haiti) about 1745 to an African woman and a French merchant-sailor. After working for a time as a seaman on his father's ships, DuSable went to France to be educated. There he developed a love for European art. At one time he may have owned several art treasures.

When DuSable returned from France, he traveled to New Orleans. Then, working as a trapper and fur trader, he made his way up the Mississippi River to St. Louis. At that time, England, Spain, and France were all trying to gain control of the new territories in North America. When the British took over the city of St. Louis, they began harassing people of French background. So DuSable moved farther north to Peoria, Illinois.

In 1769, while on a trip to Canada, DuSable stopped at a place the Potawatomi Indians called "Checagou." Recognizing the unique advantages offered by Checagou's location, he set up a trading post on the marshy shores of the river. His instincts were good. Checagou later flourished and became known as Chicago. Today, it is one of the world's greatest centers of trade and commerce.

DuSable's trading post prospered, in part, because he was able to speak English, French, Spanish, and several Native American languages. More importantly, he had developed a special relationship with various Indian groups living in the Illinois territory. His remarkable ability to work with diverse groups and interest them in his business venture added to his success.

Before long, the post expanded to include a horse stable, workshop, bakery, dairy, smokehouse, barn, and several other buildings. Within a short time, it became the main supply station for trappers, traders, and Native Americans, and was the key route for merchant trading in Detroit and Canada. Among the many products DuSable supplied were furs, meats, wheat, and bread.

Although DuSable had become a successful trader, his French background continued to cause him problems, and he was arrested twice because of it. However, British governor Patrick Sinclair was so impressed with DuSable's abilities that he asked him to take charge of a settlement on the St. Clair River. DuSable did so, and at the same time, acquired considerable property in Peoria.

In 1784, DuSable returned to Chicago with his wife Catherine, who was a Potawatomi Indian, and their children. Then in 1800, for reasons unknown, he sold his Chicago properties for only $1,200 and moved to St. Charles, Missouri, where his granddaughter lived. He died there in 1818, almost penniless, and was buried in St. Charles Borromeo Cemetery. Although he was not honored during his lifetime, Jean Baptiste Pointe DuSable had laid the foundation for one of the largest and most important cities of the world.

Crispus Attucks

Sailor, Patriot

1723—1770

"The first to defy and the first to die . . ." So reads a line of poetry about Crispus Attucks who, with four other men, was shot to death during a fight with British soldiers in the Massachusetts Bay Colony in 1770. This fight later became known as the Boston Massacre.

Born a slave of African and Natick Indian heritage, Attucks ran away from his owner, William Brown of Framingham, Massachusetts, when he was twenty-seven years old. He signed on as a sailor on a departing boat and spent the next twenty years of his life working on cargo and whaling ships. While at sea, he taught himself to read and write.

The rough, free life of a sailor suited Attucks. He was strong, brave, and quick to take the lead in difficult situations, especially those that threatened his freedom or the freedom of others. It was quite natural for him, therefore, to side with Boston colonists when they refused to obey England's oppressive laws and restrictions.

In Boston, the situation had become so tense that the British were stationing troops there to keep colonists under control. Since 1765, there had been numerous scuffles and fights between British soldiers and American patriots. On March 5, 1770, what began as a minor scuffle became a major incident on the road to revolution.

A British soldier fires at Crispus Attucks during the Boston Massacre.

Hugh Montgomery, a British soldier who was standing guard outside the Custom House, struck a young boy who had insulted him. The boy ran crying through the streets. Immediately, an angry crowd, led by Attucks, appeared and began pelting Montgomery with snowballs and pieces of ice. Soon, twelve more soldiers from the British 29th Regiment appeared, armed with muskets and bayonets.

When the crowd saw the soldiers, they hesitated. But Attucks charged ahead waving a heavy stick. "Don't be afraid. Knock 'em over. They dare not fire," he cried. Unfortunately, he was wrong. Faced with the angry crowd, the soldiers panicked. They fired into the mob, killing Attucks and Samuel Grey instantly and wounding nine other men, three of whom died.

Public reaction seesawed between shock and anger. Attucks's body lay in state in Boston's Faneuil Hall for three days. Thousands attended his funeral, and all shops in the city closed. Seven British soldiers and their commander were tried for murder but found innocent.

The Boston Massacre marked a major turning point in the events leading to the American Revolution. As John Adams later wrote, "On that night, the foundations of American Independence were laid." It is noteworthy that those "foundations" rested in part on the courage and leadership of a runaway slave named Crispus Attucks.

Benjamin Banneker

Inventor, Mathematician, Astronomer, Surveyor
1731–1806

The color of the skin is in no way connected with strength of the mind or intellectual powers.

—Benjamin Banneker

Benjamin Banneker was born on November 9, 1731, on a farm near Baltimore, Maryland. His grandmother, Molly Walsh, was an Englishwoman and former indentured servant. She acquired some land and bought an African slave named Banneka (or Bannka), whom she married. Their daughter, Mary, following her mother's example, purchased and married a slave named Robert. Mary and Robert adopted the family name, Bannak (later changed to Banneker), and acquired a farm of their own.

Using an old Bible, Molly Walsh taught young Benjamin to read and write. At age twelve he began attending a nearby Quaker school, where he showed a strong interest in mathematics. He often made up math problems just for the fun of solving them.

When Banneker was about nineteen, he met Josef Levi, a traveling salesman, who showed him a pocket watch. Banneker had never seen one before and was fascinated. When he got home, he drew up plans and made the necessary calculations to make one himself. Two years later, it was finished. Each wooden gear had been carved by hand. The first clock made in America with non-imported parts, it kept perfect time for more than forty years.

By the time of the American Revolution, Banneker had begun a serious study of astronomy. Quickly mastering the science, he predicted a solar eclipse for April 14, 1789. Two leading astronomers disagreed with his calculations, but Banneker's prediction turned out to be correct.

In 1792, Banneker began publishing an almanac. In addition to listing holidays and eclipses, it provided weather and medical information, the times of sunrise and sunset, and a tide table for the Chesapeake Bay. His almanacs also included poems and antislavery essays.

When the decision was made to move the nation's capital from Philadelphia to Washington, D.C., in 1791, Banneker, on the recommendation of Thomas Jefferson, was appointed to the civil engineering team that was planning the layout of the new city. Though almost sixty years old and in poor health, Banneker spent long hours compiling necessary data, recording astronomical observations, and maintaining the team's field astronomical clock. He also helped determine the sites for the White House, the Capitol, the Treasury, and other public buildings.

Although Banneker was preoccupied with matters of mathematics and astronomy, he was also concerned about the condition of African-Americans throughout the country. In 1791, he wrote a letter to Thomas Jefferson, criticizing Jefferson's statement, "Blacks are inferior to whites," and included a copy of his almanac to prove his point. Jefferson was impressed, and he sent a copy of the almanac to the French Academy of Sciences in Paris. Banneker's almanac was also shown in Britain's House of Commons to support the argument that African-Americans could—and should—be educated. A man far ahead of his time, Banneker died on October 25, 1806.

Phillis Wheatley

Poet

1753—1784

Should you, my lord, while you peruse my song,
Wonder from whence my love of Freedom sprung,
Whence flow these wishes for the common good,
By feeling hearts alone best understood,
I, young in life, by seeming cruel fate
Was snatch'd from Afric's fancy'd happy seat.

These are the words of Phillis Wheatley, an African-born woman who was kidnapped by slave traders when she was about eight years old and brought to Boston, Massachusetts, in 1761. There she was bought by John Wheatley, a wealthy merchant tailor, as a lady's maid for his wife Susannah.

A small, frail child, Wheatley was well cared for. Very intelligent, she learned English quickly and was taught to read. When she was fourteen, she began writing poetry. Her first work to receive widespread attention was "On the Death of the Rev. Mr. George Whitefield."

When Wheatley's health began to fail in 1772, John Wheatley freed her and sent her to England. While there, she impressed several members of the nobility. They arranged for her book, *Poems on Various Subjects, Religious and Moral,* to be published. Many prominent Massachusetts men, including John Hancock, signed the foreword of her book.

Arrangements were made for Wheatley to be introduced to the king and queen of England. Before the meeting took take place, she received word that her former mistress, Susannah, was ill, so she quickly returned to America.

When Susannah died in 1774, Wheatley remained with the family and kept house for John. She continued to write and, in 1775, published a poem dedicated to George Washington in Thomas Paine's *Pennsylvania Magazine*. Washington was so impressed that he invited her to visit him at his head-quarters in Cambridge, Massachusetts.

After John's death in 1778, Wheatley was forced to leave the house where she had grown up. Shortly thereafter, she married John Peters. He was frequently away, and the marriage was unhappy. Although in ill health, Wheatley had to work as a servant to support herself. Two of her three children died shortly after they were born. On December 5, 1784, Wheatley passed away at age thirty-one. Her third child died the same day.

Wheatley is remembered today because of her role in the development of African-American literature. In an era of great prejudice, her sensitive poetry proved that blacks were equal to whites both intellectually and emotionally. At a time when the fight against slavery often seemed endless, Wheatley's poems provided both hope and ammunition.

Peter Salem

Revolutionary War Soldier
1750–1816

"We hold these truths to be self-evident, that all men are created equal...." To thousands of African-American Revolutionary War soldiers like Peter Salem, this statement from the Declaration of Independence was more than just pretty words—it was a promise they expected the new nation to keep.

In June 1775, fifteen hundred Americans faced two to three thousand British Redcoats at the famous Battle of Bunker Hill. Three times the British charged; twice they were forced back. The third time, a British officer, Major John Pitcairn, pressed forward, shouting, "The day is ours!" Those were his last words, for it was then that Salem, an African-American soldier, killed Pitcairn with a shot to the chest. The British won the fight when the Americans' ammunition ran out, but by then it didn't matter. The American Revolution was under way.

Salem almost missed the Battle of Bunker Hill. Because many white people feared slave rebellions, it was decided in May 1775 that only free African-Americans would be accepted as soldiers. Although Salem had fought earlier at Concord and Lexington, under the new ruling he was not allowed to serve in the American army. Luckily, Salem and many other slaves were freed so they could fight. Once free, Salem immediately enlisted in Colonel Nixon's Fifth Massachusetts Regiment—just in time to fight at Bunker Hill in June.

Even free African-American fighters made some whites uneasy. So, under pressure from the Continental Congress, General George Washington issued an order that banned all African-American soldiers from fighting. The British decided to take advantage of the situation and offered freedom to all slaves willing to fight for England. When Washington heard about England's offer, he immediately reversed his decision and allowed African-Americans to enlist. As a result, more than five thousand African-Americans volunteered their services. Black soldiers fought in every major battle of the Revolutionary War.

These African-American soldiers fought bravely in the hope that, with the defeat of England, slavery would be abolished throughout the colonies. They fought not only for their own freedom but also for that of their families and friends. Their efforts were not totally in vain: by the end of the war, over sixty thousand slaves had been set free—some because they had helped fight, others because many northern states did outlaw slavery at this time.

Peter Salem fought not only at Concord, Lexington, and Bunker Hill, but also at Saratoga and Stony Point. He remained in the Continental Army until about 1780 and then settled down in Leicester, Massachusetts. In 1816, he died in a Framingham poorhouse.

James Armistead

Revolutionary War Spy
1760—1832

James Armistead was twenty-one years old when his master, William Armistead of New Kent County, Virginia, gave him permission to serve with the colonial army in the Revolutionary War. He was assigned to assist the Marquis de Lafayette, a young French general who had volunteered to fight with the Americans.

In 1791, Lafayette headed a small, ragged army of about twelve hundred men in Virginia. His orders were to bring pressure on two British armies: one led by Lord Charles Cornwallis, and the other under the command of Benedict Arnold, the American traitor who had joined the British. At the time, almost the entire state of Virginia was under British control.

Because Lafayette's tattered troops were not strong enough to meet the British in a full-scale battle, Lafayette was forced to tag along behind the Redcoats and engage them in small skirmishes. While following the British, Lafayette received orders from George Washington to find out what the enemy was planning for the coming months. He assigned Armistead to go undercover as a spy.

Armistead appeared at Benedict Arnold's headquarters shortly afterward and offered his services as a servant and guide. In return, Armistead asked to be freed when the British won the war. Arnold agreed. Quickly gaining Arnold's trust, Armistead began sending secret reports back to Lafayette detailing British positions. When Arnold was reassigned, Armistead began working for Lord Cornwallis.

In April, Cornwallis suddenly disappeared with his troops. Armistead was able to provide Americans with his location: Yorktown on the York River near Chesapeake Bay. This was the news Lafayette had been waiting for. He joined forces with Washington's troops, and together they set out to trap the British between the American army on land and the French fleet sailing toward Chesapeake Bay. The plan worked. Cornwallis was surrounded. On October 19, 1781, after ten days of fighting and negotiating, the British surrendered. The American Revolution ended with the Battle of Yorktown—an American victory due, in part, to the valuable intelligence work of Armistead.

As a reward for his services, Armistead was freed by the General Assembly of Virginia and later granted a yearly pension of $40 for the rest of his life. He changed his last name to Lafayette in recognition of his friendship with his former commander. General Lafayette, in turn, became active in efforts to abolish slavery and obtain equal rights for African-Americans.

Elizabeth Freeman

Abolitionist
1742–1829

It took the entire U.S. Army to destroy slavery in the South, but just one determined African-American woman to end it in Massachusetts.

Elizabeth Freeman grew up at a time when the American colonies were becoming more and more dissatisfied with British rule. In 1776, the Declaration of Independence was written, and everyone was talking about freedom, liberty, and equality. The home of Colonel John Ashley, where Freeman and her sister were slaves, was no different.

As Freeman served meals to the Ashley family, she listened to their discussions and drew a few conclusions of her own. Many people felt the new ideas about equality did not apply to slaves, but Freeman did. Once the fighting of the Revolutionary War ended in October 1781, she decided to take action. She left the Ashley household and refused to return. Instead, she approached a young lawyer named Theodore Sedgwick and asked him to help her gain her freedom. Sedgwick listened with interest as she argued that, according to the Declaration of Independence and the new Massachusetts Constitution adopted in 1780, she should be free. Convinced that she had a case, Sedgwick decided to represent her.

In 1781, Freeman's case was heard by the county court in Great Barrington, Massachusetts. There she claimed that, as a result of the American Revolution, slavery was illegal and she should not have to return to the Ashley household. The jury agreed. Freeman was given her freedom, and the judge ordered Colonel Ashley to pay her thirty shillings in damages. As a result of Freeman's case, slavery ended in the state of Massachusetts.

After her victory, Freeman went to work for the Sedgwick family. She died on December 28, 1829.

Richard Allen

Religious Leader, Abolitionist
1760–1831

We were stolen from our mother country and brought here. We have tilled the ground and made fortunes for thousands.

—Richard Allen

One morning in November 1787, Richard Allen and two friends, Absalom Jones and William White, were pulled from their knees while praying in St. George's Episcopal Church in Philadelphia and told that, because they were black, they must stay in the rear of the gallery. Rather than do this, the three men walked out, followed by other African-American members of the congregation.

Allen was born a slave in Philadelphia and sold along with his family to Mr. Stockley in Dover, Delaware. While living with the Stockleys, Allen taught himself to read and write and began attending Methodist church meetings. Working as a day laborer and bricklayer, he managed to save enough money to purchase his freedom in 1783.

For the next few years, Allen traveled with a Methodist minister and was occasionally allowed to preach to mixed congregations. Returning to Philadelphia in 1786, he began holding prayer meetings for African-American congregations. Shortly afterward, the incident at St. George's took place.

Following the walkout, Allen and Jones organized the Free African Society, a group that opposed slavery, and laid plans for the construction of an African-American church. Their plans were interrupted, however, when a serious yellow fever epidemic hit Philadelphia, killing hundreds of people. Allen and Jones arranged for members of the city's African-American community to serve as nurses and undertakers.

After the epidemic had run its course, Allen continued with his plans for an African-American church. Working as a shoemaker, he saved enough money to buy a lot and begin construction. On July 17, 1794, the Bethel African Methodist Episcopal Church was founded.

In 1816, Bethel cut its ties to the Methodist Church. By uniting Bethel with other African Methodist churches, Allen helped create the African Methodist Episcopal Church (AME). He became its first bishop. Eventually, it would include thousands of members throughout the country and become a national organization.

In 1795, Allen opened a school for African-American children. He also led the African-American community in petitioning the Pennsylvania legislature to abolish slavery. When the British threatened to invade Philadelphia in 1812, he and Absalom Jones helped raise twenty-five hundred African-American troops to defend the city.

Churches became a vital part of African-American life in the United States. They provided a training ground for African-American leaders and unified the efforts of the African-American community to oppose slavery and racial discrimination. This tradition of community involvement continues today.

During the Civil Rights Movement of the 1950s and 1960s, African-American ministers and their congregations took the lead in supporting efforts to end racial segregation. As a result, many black churches were dynamited or firebombed. But the African-American church has always prevailed— thanks in part to men like Richard Allen.

Gabriel Prosser

Slave Rebellion Leader
1776–1800

Of the hundreds of slave uprisings that occurred in the United States, one of the most important was led by twenty-four-year-old Gabriel Prosser. Known as the Great Gabriel Conspiracy, the rebellion took place in 1800. With his brothers, Martin and Solomon, and more than a thousand slave followers, Prosser organized the revolt, obtained weapons, and worked out the final details of the plot.

Prosser's idea was to seize Richmond and thereby encourage slave uprisings all over Virginia and the South. The slaves planned to meet on August 30 in Old Brook Swamp, 6 miles (9.7 kilometers) from the city. There they would divide into three groups: one group would attack the armory, another would take the powder house, and the third would set fires to divert attention from the others.

On that Saturday night a huge storm arose, destroying roads, wiping out bridges, and making travel impossible. Brook Swamp was flooded, and only a few hundred slaves were able to get to the meeting place. Meanwhile, two slaves became frightened and confessed the plot on the day it was to take place. Governor James Monroe placed Richmond on full alert and sent troops to apprehend Prosser and his men.

As the full plan became known, panic swept over the city. About forty slaves were executed during the next few weeks. Prosser was captured and questioned, but in spite of numerous beatings, he refused to name his followers. Tried and condemned to hang, Prosser went to his death in silence on October 7, 1800.

York

Explorer, Scout, Interpreter
1770–1832

In 1803, President Thomas Jefferson authorized the purchase of 875,000 square miles (2.27 million square km) of unexplored territory. The new land, previously owned by France, became known as the Louisiana Purchase. It stretched from Louisiana in the south to Canada in the north, and from the Mississippi River in the east to the Rocky Mountains in the west. The purchase doubled the size of the United States and opened up the West to settlement. Thirteen states would be carved from it.

Congress authorized a special expedition, under the leadership of Meriwether Lewis and William Clark, to explore the vast new land. In the spring of 1804, the expedition started out. Among the 45 men and one woman in the party was a 23-year-old man named York. He was Clark's personal slave and friend since childhood. Standing more than 6 feet (1.8 meters) tall and weighing more than 200 pounds (91 kilograms), York was an imposing figure. He was strong, athletic, and a successful hunter with an extensive knowledge of woodlore. Because he was able to speak some French and several Native American languages, he also served as an interpreter.

The expedition was guided by a French trapper named Toussaint Charbonneau. His wife, a Shoshone Indian woman named Sacajawea (or "Bird Woman") was translator. When the expedition encountered Native Americans, Sacajawea told her husband what they were saying. He, in turn, repeated it in French to York, who translated the French into English for Lewis and Clark.

Native Americans were fascinated by York. Most had never seen a man of his size, skin color, and agility. The Flathead people thought he had painted himself with charcoal, as their warriors did when they were victorious in battle.

The expedition reached the Pacific Ocean at the mouth of the Columbia River in November 1805, then returned to St. Louis, Missouri, on September 23, 1806. The members of the party faced incredible hardships during their two-and-a-half-year journey. In all, they traveled more than 8,000 miles (12,800 km) through territory that now includes the states of Missouri, Nebraska, Kansas, Montana, Idaho, Iowa, Washington, Oregon, and North and South Dakota. The first people to cross North America to the Pacific Ocean, they brought back vital information about the terrain, the plants and animals, and the location of Native American tribes.

After the expedition, Clark freed York, who returned to Kentucky to be near his wife, a slave of a local family. His skills as a scout and interpreter contributed significantly to the success of the historic Lewis and Clark expedition. The Louisiana Purchase had cost the U.S. government about $15 million. York's presence helped ensure it was money well spent.

Denmark Vesey

Slave Rebellion Leader
1767–1822

In 1799, a slave named Denmark Vesey won $1,500 with a lottery ticket and used $600 of it to pay for his freedom. In 1822, he tried to gain the freedom of every slave in Charleston, South Carolina. This time he paid with his life.

For almost twenty years, Vesey had been the property of a sea captain named Joseph Vesey. When he finally bought his freedom, Vesey set up his own carpentry shop and gradually became wealthy. He was outspoken about the evils of slavery, frequently encouraging slaves and free African-Americans to stand up for their rights. Finally, he decided the time had come for action. In 1821, he planned a massive slave revolt.

Vesey selected the leaders for his revolt carefully: Peter Poyas, cool, courageous, and a born organizer; Gullah Jack, an African-born magic man, feared and respected by many slaves; and Ned and Rolla Bennett, slaves belonging to South Carolina's governor. Vesey's strike force would eventually grow to include nine thousand people.

He planned the revolt for Sunday, July 14, 1822. His army would move at midnight, striking various key points in the city. But his plan was never carried out. A house slave who had been asked to join the revolt betrayed it instead. Because of Vesey's secret method of operation, the house slave did not know the names of the leaders of the revolt. But he knew enough. Charleston city officials acted quickly.

When Vesey heard they had been betrayed, he changed the date of the uprising to June 16, but it was too late. Another slave had gone to the authorities and confessed. Fearing capture, Vesey went into hiding but was arrested on June 22. Five days later, he was tried and convicted. The judge handed down the death sentence.

On July 2, 1822, at 6:00 A.M., Vesey was hanged along with Peter Poyas and four other followers. Eventually, thirty-seven other African-Americans were put to death for their part in the conspiracy. For Vesey, personal freedom had not been enough. He gave his life so that others could be free.

Black Seminoles

Before Florida became a state, it served as a haven for several hundred runaway slaves. A settlement known as Fort Negro became a symbol of freedom to slaves in Georgia, and many ran away hoping to find safety there. As a result, Fort Negro was destroyed in 1816 by army troops under the command of General Andrew Jackson, who later became the seventh U.S. president. The destruction of Fort Negro marked the beginning of the Seminole Wars, a series of three wars that stretched over forty years and cost the U.S. government more than $30 million.

Although the conflict is named for the Seminole people, it was, in the words of General Thomas Sidney Jesup, "a Negro and not an Indian War." The Seminoles had long offered protection to escaped slaves, and hundreds of runaway African-Americans had settled among them over the years. Often, they intermarried and became active in tribal affairs.

Runaway slaves often banded together and, with Native Americans' help, would return later to raid Georgia plantations in an effort to free friends and relatives. To stop this practice, slaveholders put pressure on the U.S. government to take control of Florida and recapture the runaway slaves. In 1819, Spain ceded Florida to the United States in exchange for $5 million worth of claims that American citizens held against Spain. Still, resistance among the Seminoles and their African-American allies remained strong. Although greatly outnumbered, they continued to engage in hit-and-run guerrilla warfare, eventually taking the lives of fifteen hundred U.S. soldiers. In 1823, however, the Seminoles were forced to accept a treaty restricting them to reservations in southern Florida.

From the beginning, African-American men such as Abraham, John Caesar, and John Horse served as important advisors and negotiators for Seminole chiefs. Abraham, an escaped slave, advised Seminole Chief Micanopy. He accompanied him to Washington, D.C., in 1825 and later helped negotiate the Treaty of Fort Gibson.

In 1835, the Second Seminole War broke out when the African-American wife of Chief Osceola was kidnapped by a government agent and sold into slavery. African-Americans were heavily involved in the conflict. When General Jesup's troops overran a Seminole camp in 1837, they captured fifty-five members of Osceola's personal guard. Of these, fifty-two were African-American. Once again, Abraham took a leading role in both military and diplomatic activities. Partly because of his negotiations, the Seminoles agreed to the 1837 Treaty of Fort Dade and left Florida for Native American territory in Oklahoma.

John Caesar had lived among the Seminoles most of his life and was an advisor to King Phillip (Emathla), second chief of the Seminole Nation after Micanopy. Caesar took the lead in encouraging resistance among the plantation slaves in the St. Johns River area. Because of his influence, the U.S. government agreed to allow African-Americans to move west with their Seminole allies. Although this guaranteed the freedom of many runaway slaves, the government cooperated because it lessened the danger of slave uprisings on Florida and Georgia plantations.

John Horse, a Native American, was a signer of the Treaty of Fort Dade. When the United States violated the treaty, he joined Osceola in renewing hostilities. While meeting with U.S. Army officials under a flag of truce, Horse, Osceola, Wild Cat, and other Seminole leaders were taken prisoner and jailed. Together with Wild Cat, Horse led a daring mass prison escape. Chased by a force of nearly a thousand men, they evaded capture and defeated the American army led by Colonel Zachary Taylor at the Battle of Lake Okeechobee. Later, John Horse led a group of black Seminoles into Mexico, where they were allowed to settle in return for guarding the border against rustlers and bandits.

Ironically, the U.S. Army, which had spent more than forty years fighting the black Seminoles, hired many of them after the Civil War. Three black Seminoles won the Congressional Medal of Honor. Long considered the best hunters, trackers, scouts, and fighters in the business, the black Seminoles were a major force in bringing law and order to the Texas-Mexico border.

Nat Turner

Slave Rebellion Leader
1800–1831

I would never be of any service to anyone as a slave.

—Nat Turner

In February 1831, there was an eclipse of the sun. Nat Turner, a man in Southampton County, Virginia, took it as a sign from God that he should lead a huge slave uprising to free those held in bondage.

Gathering together his closest friends, Turner made plans for a revolt that would take place on the Fourth of July. As the day approached, however, he became ill. Canceling the plans, the men waited for another sign. On August 13, 1831, a bluish-green haze covered the sun. Interpreting this as the sign they had been waiting for, Turner and six followers met again to work out the final details of the uprising.

On August 22, the revolt began. The first house to be attacked belonged to Turner's owner, Joseph Travis. Travis, his wife and child, and two other people were killed. For 40 hours the revolt continued. Between 60 and 80 slaves joined the rebellion. They killed at least 57 slaveholders and their families, sparing only poor white people who did not own slaves.

When the word of the revolt reached the authorities, hundreds of armed white men rode off in search of Turner. Dozens of rebel slaves, carrying only a few weapons, were killed or captured. Turner evaded authorities for two months. Finally, on October 30, 1831, the Virginia militia captured him. On November 5, he was tried, found guilty, and sentenced to death. Six days later he was hanged, and his body was disposed of secretly.

Although the revolt was over, reaction to it was just beginning. Of those formally charged with participating in the uprising, twenty-four were either acquitted or freed for lack of evidence. Twenty-nine were convicted; seventeen of these, including Turner, were hanged. Approximately two hundred other African-Americans were killed by slave owners determined to terrify the remaining African-American population into submission.

The white community was shocked by the revolt. They could not believe that Turner, of all people, had led it. Far from having a reputation as a violent or difficult slave, Turner had been a deeply religious man. Known as "The Prophet," he had preached on Sundays and was highly respected by both black and white communities.

Turner went to his death with dignity and courage. He once said that on the day he was to die, the sun would refuse to shine as a sign from God that slavery was evil. Not everyone took Turner's religious pronouncement seriously, but the local sheriff did. He refused to cut the rope that would spring the trap on the gallows. No one else was anxious to do it either, so an old man was brought from out of town to act as an executioner. While the sun didn't exactly refuse to shine, the sky did go dark when a major thunderstorm arose on the day of the hanging. Thunderstorms in November are a bit unusual, and many people found the coincidence unsettling.

Joseph Cinque (Sengbe Pieh)

Leader of Slave Ship Uprising
1817–1879

"Give us free. Give us free." Though he spoke very little English, there was no doubt as to what Joseph Cinque wanted. He had seized control of a slave ship and freed approximately fifty African men and four children. Now he was being charged with mutiny and murder in a New Haven, Connecticut, courtroom.

The story began when Cinque was kidnapped by slave traders in April 1839 and sold to the owner of a slave factory at Lomboko on the African coast. From there he was shipped to Havana, Cuba, on a Portuguese slave ship under conditions so terrible that half the slaves on board died.

It was illegal to bring new slaves into Cuba at the time, so upon their arrival in Havana, Cinque and the rest of the slave "cargo" were sold secretly to a planter named Ruiz. Together with another slave owner named Montés, Ruiz transferred the slaves to a ship called the *Amistad,* which set sail for a sugar plantation on the island of Principe.

Desperate to escape, Cinque managed to pry a rusty nail out of the ship's side and used it to unfasten the chain that bound him and the other captives. The newly freed slaves then crept up on deck, where they killed the captain and most of the crew and captured Ruiz and Montés. Since the Africans knew nothing about sailing a ship that size, they were forced to rely on their captives. Ordered to sail east for Africa, Montés tricked Cinque by changing direction at night so that the ship headed north.

Ruiz and Montés had hoped to reach the southern United States, where slavery was legal. Instead, they landed north near Montauk Point on Long Island. When Cinque and some of the other Africans went ashore to find food and water, a U.S. Coast Guard ship, U.S.S. *Washington,* appeared and forced the *Amistad* to surrender. Upon his return to the ship, Cinque was arrested. He and the others were charged with mutiny and murder.

The Spanish and Cuban authorities demanded that the United States return both the ship and the slaves to them. But U.S. abolitionists protested. Ruiz and Montés were the real criminals, they said, not Cinque and the other Africans.

Cinque's trial was held on January 7, 1840, in New Haven, Connecticut. It created a sensation. Classes at Yale Law School were dismissed so that students could attend the trial. Although Cinque and the others could not speak English, they argued through an interpreter that they had been kidnapped and had the right to resist by any means necessary. The court agreed, but the case was appealed. On September 17, 1840, the circuit court of appeals upheld the lower court's decision. However, President Martin Van Buren, sympathetic to southern slaveholders, ordered the U.S. Justice Department to appeal the case once again—this time to the U.S. Supreme Court.

At this point, former president John Quincy Adams agreed to represent the Africans. Though he was then in his seventies and almost blind, Adams was still active in the antislavery movement. After an eight-and-a-half-hour argument before the court, Adams won the case. On March 9, 1841, Cinque and the others were ordered freed without delay. In November they returned to Africa, settling in Sierra Leone. Cinque died in 1879.

Mutinies on slave ships were not uncommon, due in part to the terrible treatment the slaves received. Chained together and packed into filthy ship holds under conditions so crowded that it was almost impossible to move, slaves died by the thousands. Estimates of men, women, and children believed to have been imported from Africa to North and South America and the Caribbean between 1500 and 1870 range from 9,566,100 to 13,887,500. In the late 1700s, when the trade was at its peak, an average of 80,000 people a year fell victim to slave traders. Of these, 12.5 percent to 14.5 percent died before ever reaching the Americas. Some died from beatings; others committed suicide. Most succumbed to disease—dysentery, fever, and smallpox—brought on by the filthy, unsanitary conditions they were forced to endure.

In 1807, the U.S. government outlawed the importation of slaves, but enforcement was weak. The trade continued illegally, and thousands of Africans were smuggled in every year. It took the Civil War to end slavery in the United States—and the African slave trade that went with it.

James Pierson Beckwourth

Frontiersman, Scout, Explorer
1798–1866

Born in Fredericksburg, Virginia, to a black slave mother and English father, James Pierson Beckwourth and his family later moved to Missouri. When he was nineteen, he was taken to St. Louis to learn a trade. In 1822, after getting into a fight with his master, Beckwourth took off for New Orleans. There he signed up as a scout for General William Henry Ashley's Rocky Mountain Fur Company.

Before long, Beckwourth had become a famous mountain man, respected for his expert skill with a knife and gun. In 1824, he was adopted by the Crow nation and married a Crow woman named Pine Leaf. His remarkable courage earned him the name "Bloody Arm."

Beckwourth remained with the Crow Indians for six years, then returned to St. Louis, where he joined the army. After serving as a scout during the Second (or Western) Seminole War (1835–42), he traveled to California, where he prospected for gold. While working as a chief scout for General John Frémont, Beckwourth discovered an important pass through the Sierra Nevada Mountains. The passage, now known as Beckwourth Pass, became an important route for wagon trains traveling west into California.

In 1866, the U.S. government asked Beckwourth to use his influence to establish peaceful relations with the Crow. Happy to see him again, the Crow asked him to return to the tribe as a chief. Beckwourth declined. The Indians prepared a farewell feast to honor him. However, when he sat down to enjoy the festivities, it turned out to be the last meal he ever ate. Legend has it that the Crow poisoned him, believing that if they could not have him alive, they could at least keep his body and powerful spirit with them. If the legend is true, the Crow meant to bestow a great honor on Beckwourth— one he probably would have preferred to do without.

Norbert Rillieux

Inventor
1806–1894

On March 17, 1806, Norbert Rillieux was born in New Orleans, Louisiana. He was the son of a hardworking plantation slave and a wealthy French engineer.

As a young man, Rillieux was given his freedom and sent to Paris, where he studied engineering at L'Ècole Centrale. At age twenty-four, he became an instructor there, specializing in steam engine technology. He also developed a theory called multiple-effect evaporation, which he applied to the process of sugar refining.

Previously, sugar had been obtained from sugarcane during a slow and expensive process called the "Jamaica Train." Groups of men (usually slaves) continually poured boiling sugarcane juice from one kettle to another until it was brown and lumpy. Rillieux designed a multiple-effect vacuum pan evaporator that improved the quality of the sugar and produced it at a much lower cost. Soon his machine was in great demand in the United States, Mexico, Cuba, and Caribbean countries.

Today, Rillieux's theories still form the basis for manufacturing sugar, soap, glue, gelatin, and condensed milk. Brilliant, hardworking, and proud, Rillieux produced, in the words of Charles Browne, a U.S. Department of Agriculture chemist, "[an] invention [that] is the greatest in the history of American chemical engineering."

The Underground Railroad

It was called the Underground Railroad, but it didn't run on tracks. It was a secret escape system for runaway slaves. Those using the railroad needed courage and determination, not tickets. Runaways traveled through fields and swamps, woods and back country roads; across rivers, creeks, and mountains; by boat, wagon, horse, train, and on foot. Sometimes they headed north toward Canada, sometimes west toward Mexico, and sometimes south toward Spanish-owned Florida, the Bahamas, and the free islands of the

Levi Coffin, known as the "President of the Underground Railroad"

Caribbean. Yet no matter what direction these men and women headed, their destination was always the same—freedom.

From the beginning, there was resistance to slavery. This resistance grew stronger with the signing of the Declaration of Independence, proclaiming freedom as an inalienable right. In 1777, Vermont became the first colony to abolish slavery. The following year, the Continental Congress forbade slavery in the Northwest Territory. By 1804, slavery had been outlawed partially or completely in most northeastern states.

Although the slave system remained strong throughout the South, efforts to end it continued, forcing Congress to forbid the importation of new slaves into the United States after January 1, 1808. The pressure to end slavery came from white people and free African-Americans known as abolitionists. This group included individuals such as Benjamin Franklin, Thomas Paine, and the Marquis de Lafayette. Abolitionists made hundreds of speeches, organized dozens of antislavery meetings, and repeatedly petitioned the president and other political leaders to end slavery.

Those people willing to help slaves escape became agents of the Underground Railroad. They included human rights leaders Frederick Douglass, Harriet Tubman, Sojourner Truth, William Lloyd Garrison, Susan B. Anthony, Congressman Thaddeus Stevens, famous detective Allen Pinkerton, writers Henry David Thoreau and Harriet Beecher Stowe, and poet John Greenleaf Whittier.

Some of these people, such as Tubman, acted as "conductors," slipping deep into slave territory to meet with runaways and guide them to safety. Others, such as Douglass, operated "stations" or "depots"—safe places where runaways could hide as they made their way to freedom. Jermain Loguen, once a slave himself, helped more than fifteen hundred people escape, and Levi Coffin, a Cincinnati Quaker who was called the "President of the Underground Railroad," helped more than three thousand to escape.

All of this help would have done little good had it not been for the actions of the slaves themselves. Although slaveholders insisted that their slaves were happy and contented, the opposite was true. Forced to work long hours in the hot sun, many slaves were punished harshly. Families were torn apart as husbands and wives were separated and children sold. Even slaves who were well treated resented their situation and wished to be free.

No one knows for sure how many slaves fled, though the numbers run into the thousands. We know that one man hid in a crate and had himself mailed north. Another carved a pair of wooden shoes that he wore as he walked more than 1,500 miles (2,400 km) to freedom.

Owners hired slave hunters to track down and recapture escaped slaves, and they offered money for information leading to the whereabouts of people like Harriet Tubman. In return for allowing California to enter the Union as a free state, slaveholders insisted that Congress pass the Fugitive Slave Law, which required citizens to help law officers apprehend and return escaped slaves.

Many Underground Railroad activists were sent to prison. Others, like newspaper editor Elijah Lovejoy, were murdered. But slaves continued to run away, and the Underground Railroad continued to function, until the Civil War finally ran slavery off the track.

Lewis Temple

Inventor
1800–1854

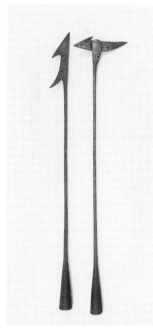

Born in Richmond, Virginia, in 1800, Lewis Temple later made his way to New Bedford, Massachusetts. Although very little is known about his early life, it is possible that he was an escaped slave. New Bedford was an important stop, or "station," on the Underground Railroad, and many runaway slaves passed through there. After settling in New Bedford in 1829, Temple opened up a blacksmith shop and married Mary Clark. By 1836, he was making harpoons, lances, and other equipment used on whaling ships.

After hearing sailors complain that whales frequently pulled loose from harpoons and escaped during a hunt, Temple designed a new instrument that would hold whales more securely. His harpoon had a movable head or "toggle" that would not come loose once it entered the whale. Far superior to the ordinary barbed-head harpoon, "Temple's Toggle," as it was called, was an immediate success. With his increased income, Temple constructed a larger shop in 1845.

Unfortunately, a few years later, Temple was badly injured as a result of city negligence. He sued the city for $2,000 but died in 1854 before he could collect any money. Temple's wife sold his shop to pay their debts, and there was little left. But whalers were left with plenty—they had Temple's Toggle, the invention that revolutionized the whaling industry.

Dred Scott

Plaintiff in Slave Lawsuit
1795–1858

In 1846, a slave named Dred Scott sued his owners for his freedom. After several trials and appeals, the case reached the U.S. Supreme Court. The final decision made history and brought the United States one step closer to the Civil War.

Scott was born a slave in Southampton County, Virginia, around 1795. After the death of his owner, Peter Blow, in 1831, he was sold to John Emerson, a U.S. Army surgeon stationed in Missouri.

In the course of his army service, Emerson was transferred to Fort Armstrong in Rock Island, Illinois. Illinois was a free state, and slavery was prohibited there. Emerson, considering himself still a resident of Missouri and living only temporarily in Illinois, believed it was legal to take his slave, Scott, with him. Two years later, Emerson was transferred to the free territory of Wisconsin. Once again, Scott accompanied him and his wife. Then, in 1839, they all returned to Missouri.

When Emerson died in 1843, Scott tried to purchase freedom for himself and his family. When Mrs. Emerson refused his request, he sued. He argued that because he had lived for several years in free territory, he should be free. Suing was not as easy as it sounds. Scott was able to file suit because Mrs. Emerson supported him in his effort, even though she felt that, for legal reasons, she could not simply free him.

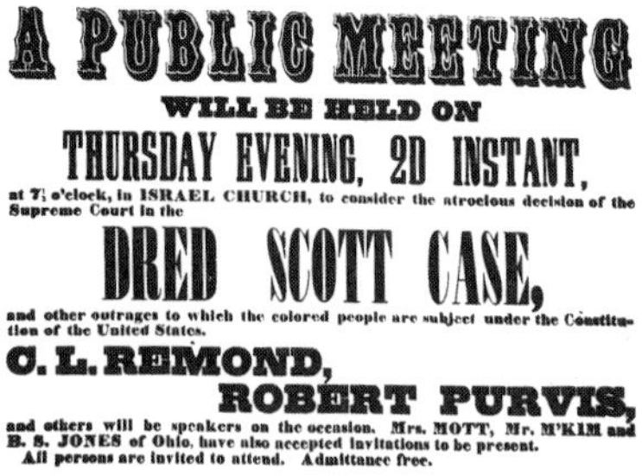

A PUBLIC MEETING
WILL BE HELD ON
THURSDAY EVENING, 2D INSTANT,
at 7½ o'clock, in ISRAEL CHURCH, to consider the atrocious decision of the Supreme Court in the
DRED SCOTT CASE,
and other outrages to which the colored people are subject under the Constitution of the United States.
C. L. REMOND,
ROBERT PURVIS,
and others will be speakers on the occasion. Mrs. MOTT, Mr. M'KIM and B. S. JONES of Ohio, have also accepted invitations to be present.
All persons are invited to attend. Admittance free.

Public meetings were held to protest the Supreme Court's decision against Dred Scott.

Scott lost his initial court battle and sued again, this time winning in a St. Louis court in 1850. The ruling, however, was overturned by the Missouri Supreme Court in 1852. With the aid of white abolitionist supporters and friends, Scott decided to appeal his case to the U.S. Supreme Court. He had little chance of victory because the chief justice, Roger B. Taney, was a southerner who favored slavery.

On March 6, 1857, the Supreme Court handed down its decision. It said that as an African-American man, Scott was not a citizen of the United States and had no right to sue anybody. Furthermore, the court ruled that Congress could not prevent slave owners from taking their property (in this case, slaves) anywhere in the country. This meant that all antislavery laws, including the Missouri Compromise that outlawed slavery north of 36° 30′ north latitude, were unconstitutional. In the words of Chief Justice Taney, African-Americans were an "inferior class of beings" who "had no rights which the white man was bound to respect."

The reaction to the U.S. Supreme Court ruling was immediate and widespread. Mass meetings were held throughout the North and West, protesting the decision. Many blacks and whites gave up hope of ever ending slavery. But Frederick Douglass, the famous abolitionist, was not discouraged. "The Supreme Court is not the only power in this world," he said. "Judge Taney cannot bail out the ocean . . . or pluck the silvery star of liberty from our Northern sky."

As for Scott, he remained in Missouri, where he died two years later. Although he had not gained his freedom, his lawsuit led to a court decision that helped bring about the Civil War four years later by ending any hope for a peaceful solution to slavery.

Lewis Hayden

Abolitionist, State Legislator
1815–1889

His mother was so badly treated that she became insane and attempted suicide. His brothers and sisters were sold at an auction, and Lewis Hayden himself was traded for a pair of carriage horses. When he finally escaped, he spent his life trying to free others.

Married while still in his teens, Hayden and his fourteen-year-old wife eventually had three children. One child died and another was sold. Although he had several opportunities to run away, it would have meant leaving his family behind—so Hayden waited.

Finally, when his son was ten years old, Hayden and his family escaped with the help of two white abolitionist teachers, Calvin Fairbank and Delia Webster. The Haydens made their way safely from Lexington, Kentucky, to Ohio and then to Canada. But Fairbank and Webster were arrested and charged with slave stealing. In February 1845, Fairbank agreed to plead guilty if Webster were allowed to go free. Webster was released, and Fairbank was sentenced to fifteen years in prison.

Meanwhile, Hayden and his family moved to Detroit, Michigan, where he established a school for African-American children. Hearing of Fairbank's imprisonment, Hayden raised $650 and sent it to his old owner. In return, his owner agreed to petition the governor of Kentucky to free Fairbank. On August 23, 1849, Fairbank was released after spending four years in prison.

Hayden then moved his family to Boston, where he became active in the Underground Railroad. His house served as the main Boston station, sheltering hundreds of runaway slaves. Among these runaways were William and Ellen Craft. On the day their owner sent slave catchers to arrest them, Hayden barricaded his house and threatened to blow it up if a slave hunter set foot inside. Meanwhile, the Crafts escaped to safety, and the slave catchers were forced to return home without them.

The following year, Hayden was arrested for helping a slave named Shadrach escape. Brought to trial, Hayden was acquitted after the jury, in spite of strong evidence, refused to convict him.

In 1854, Hayden, Reverend Thomas Wentworth Higginson, and a group of fifteen white men and ten black men tried to free Anthony Burns, a runaway slave who was being held in a Boston jail. The men broke down the courthouse door, and a wild fight took place. They were forced out of the building, however, and Burns was returned south to slavery.

When the Civil War broke out, Hayden helped recruit African-Americans for the Union army. His son enlisted in the Navy and was killed in action. Hayden spent his later years working for civil rights for African-Americans and women. He was elected to the Massachusetts legislature and arranged for a monument to be erected in the memory of the African-American Revolutionary War hero Crispus Attucks. Although there is no monument to Hayden, he, like Attucks, was a true American hero.

Harriet Ross Tubman

Underground Railroad Conductor, Abolitionist
1821–1913

On my underground railroad I never ran my train off the track. And I never lost a passenger.

—Harriet Ross Tubman

WANTED! DEAD OR ALIVE— $40,000 REWARD! This was the price slaveholders were willing to pay for Harriet Ross Tubman, an African-American woman who ran away from slavery in 1849 and spent the next sixteen years of her life trying to free others.

Born Araminta Ross in Dorchester County, Maryland, around 1821, Tubman was one of eleven children. Although highly intelligent, she was not allowed to attend school or learn to read or write. Instead, she spent her childhood working in the fields. At age fifteen or sixteen, her master threw a rock at her when she tried to protect another slave from an angry overseer. The blow almost killed her, and for the rest of her life she suffered from seizures that caused her to "black out" briefly. She also began to see visions and hear voices warning her of danger and urging her to make her way north to freedom.

When she was twenty-eight years old, Tubman did just that. Guided by the North Star, she made her way to Philadelphia. But personal freedom was not enough for Tubman. She joined the Underground Railroad and made approximately nineteen dangerous trips to the South to bring more than three hundred slaves (including her brother, sister, and aged parents) to freedom.

Tubman earned money for her rescue missions by working as a cook and laundress. When she had saved enough money, she would disguise herself and make her way south into slave territory. White people who happened to run into her saw only a harmless, half-crazy old woman, wandering along singing religious songs. What they did not know was that the songs were a code alerting slaves to her arrival.

Tubman's rules of escape were very simple: be on time; tell no one of your plans; follow commands without complaint; and, most important, be prepared to die rather than turn back. She meant what she said. Tubman often carried a gun and threatened to shoot anyone who tried to quit. No one ever did. Tubman planned her escapes for Saturday nights, to give her groups at least a 36-hour head start before angry slave owners could get their wanted posters printed on Monday.

During the Civil War, Tubman worked as a scout, spy, and nurse for the Union Army. She led a raid that resulted in the freedom of more than 750 slaves. Following the war, she attempted to establish schools for African-Americans and later worked in support of women's rights.

Tubman lived to be ninety-two. When she died, she was buried in Ohio with military honors. Flags flew at half-mast in New York as whites and blacks gathered to pay tribute to the woman they called "the general" and the "Moses of her People."

In 1974, Tubman's home in Auburn, New York, was designated a National Historic Landmark. In 1978, the U.S. Postal Service issued a Harriet Tubman stamp in honor of a rare woman who, through her courage and determination, had placed her own stamp on American history.

Jermain Wesley Loguen

Abolitionist, Minister, Underground Railroad Conductor
1813–1872

Harriet Tubman helped three hundred people escape from slavery, but she needed the help of abolitionist Jermain Wesley Loguen to gain her own freedom.

Loguen was born near Nashville, Tennessee. His mother, a free African-American, had been kidnapped and sold to David Logue. Although Logue became Jermain's father, he cared nothing about the boy or his mother and sold them both. The suffering his mother had to endure, the sale of his sister, and the brutal murder of another slave convinced Loguen to run away.

Loguen was twenty-one when he escaped north to Detroit, Michigan, and then to Canada, where he went to school. Returning to the United States, he continued his education at the Oneida Institute in New York. Later, he opened two schools for African-American children in New York. In 1842, he became an ordained Methodist minister and established the Abolition Church and five smaller churches. During this period he changed the name his father had given him, Jarm Logue, to Jermain Loguen.

Loguen strongly supported the movement to end slavery. He worked closely with Frederick Douglass and often wrote articles for Douglass's *North Star* newspaper. Loguen was also an important conductor on the

Underground Railroad. Tubman was just one of approximately fifteen hundred runaway slaves he helped to escape.

After the end of the Civil War and the passage of the Thirteenth Amendment, which ended slavery, Loguen became more active in the African Methodist Episcopal Zion Church. He is most remembered, however, for his work as an abolitionist and conductor on the Underground Railroad. At a time when such activities could have led to his imprisonment, re-enslavement, or even death, Loguen stood fast and helped fifteen hundred runaways ride the Underground Railroad's "Freedom Train."

Frederick Douglass

Abolitionist, Newspaper Editor, Orator
1817–1895

Save the Negro and you save the nation. Destroy the Negro and you destroy the nation, and to save both you must have but one great law of Liberty, Equality and Fraternity for all Americans.

—Frederick Douglass

Frederick Augustus Washington Bailey (Frederick Douglass) did not know the exact date of his birth. He picked February 14 for his birthday because his mother used to call him her "little valentine."

Born a slave in Tuckahoe, Maryland, Douglass never knew who his father was. When he was still a baby, his mother was sent to work on a plantation miles away. Sometimes, after work, she would walk 12 miles (19 km) back to see him before he went to sleep. When Douglass was about seven, she died.

Often, Douglass was so hungry that he would fight with the dog, Old Nep, for bits of discarded food. Even worse was the cold. Douglass, like other slave children, wore only a rough, knee-length shirt. In the winter, he wrapped himself in an old sack and slept on the floor.

Master Anthony's daughter, Lucretia Auld, took a liking to Douglass. At her suggestion, he was sent to Baltimore as a companion to her nephew,

Tommy Auld. There Douglass learned to read and write.

When Douglass was sixteen, he was ordered back to the plantation. One day, after refusing to obey his master, Douglass was sent to Edward Covey, a slave breaker who beat him and denied him food. Despite the danger of worse punishment, Douglass fought back.

Douglass dreamed constantly of being free. With five other men, he made plans to steal a boat, row to Chesapeake Bay, and hike north into Pennsylvania. But before their plans could be carried out, they were arrested and thrown in jail. Douglass was sent back to Baltimore, where he met and fell in love with Anna Murray, a free-born African-American woman. Together they plotted his second escape attempt.

On September 3, 1838, using the borrowed identification papers of a friendly African-American sailor, Douglass escaped by train to New York. David Ruggles, an African-American abolitionist, took him in and helped make arrangements for Anna to come to New York, where Douglass and she were married.

To avoid slave hunters, Douglass changed his last name from Bailey to Douglass. He also began speaking to audiences about his life as a slave. Soon, the Massachusetts Anti-Slavery Society asked Douglass to speak on their behalf. He was so articulate that many people began to doubt he had ever been a slave. To convince them, he wrote *Narrative of the Life of Frederick Douglass, An American Slave* (1845). Worried that information in the book would lead his owner to him, Douglass went to England.

In England, Douglass continued to lecture against slavery. He also spoke out in favor of Irish freedom, women's rights, and world peace. Numerous friends encouraged him to remain in England, but Douglass did not want to abandon African-Americans still trapped by slavery. Knowing Douglass's return would be dangerous, a group of English supporters arranged to purchase his freedom so that he could return home safely.

When Douglass returned to the United States in 1847, he settled in Rochester, New York, where he established a newspaper called the *North Star*. The name was chosen because runaway slaves heading north without compasses often used the North Star as their guide. The *North Star's* motto, "Right is of no sex—Truth is of no color—God is the Father of us all, and all we are brethren," set the tone for Douglass's writing. Although he was concerned mainly with the abolition of slavery, he also favored equal rights for women and Native Americans, supported public education, and fought to end the death penalty.

When the Civil War began, Douglass encouraged President Lincoln to free all slaves and allow them to enlist in the Union forces. After the war, Douglass held several government posts: U.S. marshal for the District of Columbia, recorder of deeds, and minister-resident and consul-general to Haiti and the Dominican Republic. After retiring from office, Douglass focused on the growing problems of segregation and lynching. But this battle was to be left to others. On February 10, 1895, he died of a heart attack.

Often considered the foremost African-American leader of the nineteenth century, Douglass has been referred to as the father of the Civil Rights Movement. An outstanding speaker, writer, political analyst, and diplomat, Douglass saw, as many others did not, that the dream of American democracy could never be fulfilled as long as slavery and injustice prevailed.

Sojourner Truth

Abolitionist, Women's Rights Activist, Preacher
1797–1883

I have borne thirteen children and seen them almost all sold off into slavery, and when I cried out with my mother's grief none but Jesus heard.

—Sojourner Truth

They called her a "Pilgrim of God" because she said the Lord had sent her to travel the countryside and "declare the truth unto people." Born in 1797, in Hurley, New York, Sojourner Truth (originally named Isabella Baumfree) sought in religion a sanctuary from the terrible cruelties she suffered as a slave. Sold four times, she ran away in 1826, two years before slavery was officially abolished in New York. With the help of a Quaker family, she won a lawsuit to have her son returned to her (he had been sold at age five to a slave owner in Alabama).

For the next few years, Truth worked in New York and attended various churches, hoping to satisfy her religious yearnings. In 1843, she said, a voice from God told her to leave the city and to take the name "Sojourner." The voice told her to "travel up and down the land showing the people their sins and being a sign unto them." When she asked the Lord for a second name, he gave her the name "Truth" because she was to tell everyone the truth about slavery.

For nearly twenty years, Truth traveled across the country speaking out on slavery and women's rights. Though not an eloquent speaker, she was dramatic and very effective. Her statements on slavery won her the respect of Frederick Douglass, William Lloyd Garrison, and other well-known abolitionists and, in 1864, she was invited to meet with Abraham Lincoln at the White House.

When the Civil War began, Truth raised money for African-American Union soldiers by lecturing and singing. In 1862, she moved to Arlington, Virginia, near Washington, D.C., to help newly freed slaves adjust to freedom. It was there that she became the first "Freedom Rider."

Until 1865, horse cars in Washington were segregated. When Congress outlawed segregation, Truth decided to test the new law. One day, after several horse cars refused to stop for her, she stood in the middle of the road, waving her arms and shouting, "I want to ride! I want to ride!" Before long, a crowd gathered and forced the next horse car to stop. Truth climbed aboard and refused to move when the conductor tried to throw her off. Unable to budge her, the conductor gave in. Truth was not quite through making her point, however. To make sure everyone was aware of the new law, she had the conductor arrested and fired.

Truth spent the remainder of her life trying to obtain land out West for newly freed slaves. She died on November 23, 1883.

Robert Smalls
Civil War Hero, Congressman
1839–1915

One of the most famous heroes of the Civil War was a twenty-three-year-old man named Robert Smalls. When the war started, Smalls was assigned to the slave crew of the Confederate dispatch ship *Planter*. On the night of May 13, 1862, the *Planter* lay anchored in the harbor at Charleston, South Carolina. Her captain, a man named Relyea, and other officers had gone ashore after spending the day hauling guns.

It was then that Smalls made his move. An expert sailor, he knew the tides, shoals, and currents and could handle the ship easily. After smuggling aboard his wife, children, and five other people, he and the eight-man crew hoisted anchor and maneuvered the *Planter* out into the main channel.

The risks were great. Fort Sumter, well-armed and in Confederate hands, overlooked Charleston harbor. Morris Island, also well-armed and under Confederate control, stood between Smalls and the Union navy. Even if he succeeded in getting past these two strongholds without being stopped, there was always the chance that the Union ships would fire on the *Planter*, not realizing it was no longer under enemy control. But Smalls was ready to take the risk.

The Confederate soldiers guarding Fort Sumter watched the *Planter* glide past. Smalls, wearing the captain's large straw hat, stood on deck with his arms folded. The soldiers, thinking he was Captain Relyea, were not suspicious at first. When they finally realized their mistake, it was too late. They tried to signal Morris Island, but the *Planter* was already in open water, out of range of Confederate guns.

When Smalls reached Union territory, he turned the *Planter* over to the Yankee fleet and joined the Union forces. Everyone was amazed at his courage and boldness. One slave was overheard saying to another, "Robert Smalls, Robert Smalls, that's all you ever talk about. Robert Smalls ain't God, you know." "Yeah, I know," said his friend, "but don't forget, Smalls is young yet."

Congress awarded Smalls and the rest of the crew one-half the appraised value of the *Planter* (Smalls received $1,500). He was made a captain in the Union navy and given command of the *Planter* until the end of the war. Afterward, he returned to South Carolina, where he was elected first to the South Carolina House of Representatives and then to the state senate. Later, he served in the U.S. Congress.

While in office, Smalls worked to pass laws that promoted African-American education and provided increased financial opportunities for them. Even though slavery had ended, many former slave owners were attempting to restrict African-American progress, first through the courts and state legislatures and, when that didn't work, through threats and violence.

Smalls was never intimidated. In 1913, at the age of seventy-three, he single-handedly saved two African-American men from being lynched. Two years later, on February 22, 1915, Smalls died in Beaufort, South Carolina.

The Emancipation Proclamation

1863

In 1858, Abraham Lincoln ran for senator of Illinois on the Republican ticket against Democrat Stephen A. Douglas. At that time, Lincoln said, "A house divided against itself cannot stand. I believe this government cannot endure, permanently, half slave and half free."

Although Lincoln lost the election, his opposition to slavery was reported widely. When he ran for president in 1860, southern Democrats threatened to secede (withdraw) from the Union if he won. He did win, and six weeks later South Carolina voted to leave the Union. Mississippi, Florida, Alabama, Georgia, Louisiana, and Texas followed. By February 1861, they had formed the Confederate States of America with Jefferson Davis as president.

Two months later, on April 12, 1861, Confederate forces under General Beauregard attacked Fort Sumter in South Carolina, and the Civil War began. Four more slave states—Virginia, North Carolina, Arkansas, and Tennessee—joined the Confederacy. The remaining slave states—Maryland, Delaware, Kentucky, and Missouri (also known as the border states)—did not. To keep their allegiance, Lincoln moved cautiously on the issue of freeing

slaves. At first, he recommended that slave owners
receive payment for freed
slaves. To calm owners' fears,
he did not allow African-
Americans to serve in the
army. As the fighting dragged
on, however, attitudes began
to change.

On January 1, 1863,
Lincoln issued the Emancipation Proclamation. The

President Abraham Lincoln reads a draft of the
Emancipation Proclamation to his cabinet.

document stated that slaves in Confederate-held territory (about three-
fourths of all slaves) were considered free, and African-Americans could
enlist in the Union forces.

The Emancipation Proclamation did not apply to the 800,000 slaves in
the four border states that had not seceded, or to those in territory under
Union control. But the proclamation still had its effect in these areas. Army
recruiters, promising freedom, encouraged thousands of slaves to run away
and enlist. This, together with growing antislavery sentiments, greatly
undermined the institution of slavery in these areas.

Issuing the Emancipation Proclamation and enforcing it were two different
things. Slavery in Confederate-controlled territory continued to exist until
Union troops took over. Still, the proclamation gave hope to thousands of
people who had fought to outlaw slavery. Allowing African-American
soldiers to enlist helped turn the tide against the South. More importantly,
the proclamation firmly placed the president and the federal government in
the position of supporting freedom for all, regardless of race.

African-American Civil War Soldiers

1861–1865

When the Civil War began in 1861, thousands of African-Americans tried to enlist in the Union army. Jacob Dodson, a black frontiersman who had served with Kit Carson and General John Frémont, offered to raise a force of three hundred African-American men to defend Washington, D.C. G. P. Miller of Michigan wrote to the secretary of war, offering to raise an army of up to ten thousand freemen. Both were turned down.

Although President Lincoln personally opposed slavery, he was concerned that if slavery were made the main issue of the war, the four slave states still in the Union would secede. He also feared many northerners would not support a war to free African-Americans. Frederick Douglass protested, calling this policy "weak and contemptible tenderness toward bloodthirsty slaveholding traitors." He could not convince Lincoln. In fact, in the early days of the war, Union troops were instructed to return runaway slaves to their owners.

Many white soldiers resisted the official slave policy. In April 1862, General David Hunter tried to arm several thousand former slaves in South Carolina, but the War Department rejected his request. General Ben Butler of Virginia was more successful. He declared captured or escaped slaves "contraband" (illegal goods) and ordered them freed. Within two months, nine hundred "contrabands" were working for the Union army.

Often, slaves helped white Union soldiers who were trapped in Confederate territory. In the words of one Union soldier, "To see a black face was to find a true heart." Many other slaves risked their lives to provide Union commanders with information about Confederate plans and operations.

As Union soldiers continued to die, pressure to allow African-Americans to serve began to build. Secretary of the Navy Gideon Welles made the first move on September 25, 1861. He authorized the enlistment of African-American sailors at $10 a month and one meal a day. A year later, the Emancipation Proclamation allowed African-Americans to enlist in the Union army. By that time black military units were already fighting in Louisiana, Missouri, and South Carolina.

Within seven months of the signing of the proclamation, more than thirty African-Americans regiments were in existence. By 1865, there were 166 all-black regiments. In all, approximately 180,000 African-American soldiers and 29,511 African-American sailors (one out of every four Navy soldiers, most of them former slaves) fought for the Union. Another 200,000 black men and women served as scouts, spies, laborers, blacksmiths, nurses, cooks, and guides.

African-American soldiers were not treated well. They were forced to serve in segregated units, almost always under the command of white officers. They often received inferior equipment and lacked medical supplies. Near the end of the war, they were still being paid only $10 a month ($3 was usually withheld to pay for uniforms and equipment), while white soldiers were getting $13. Some African-Americans protested. The men of the all-black Fifty-fourth Massachusetts Regiment refused to accept discriminatory pay and would not accept any wages for a year.

Even worse, captured African-American soldiers were often shot or sold as slaves instead of being treated as prisoners of war. On April 12, 1864, some three hundred black troops who had been forced to surrender were massacred at Fort Pillow, Tennessee. Six days later, wounded and captured African-Americans were murdered by Confederate troops at the Battle of Poison Springs, Arkansas.

President Lincoln had issued an order stating that for every African-American prisoner shot, a Confederate prisoner would be killed, and for every African-American prisoner sold into slavery, a Confederate prisoner would be subjected to forced labor. But African-American soldiers did not wait for Lincoln's retribution policy to be carried out. They fought fiercely, preferring death to surrender.

Of the disastrous Battle of Olustee in Florida, an officer of the Fifty-fourth Massachusetts Regiment writes,

> We have had a fight, a licking, and a footrace. We marched 110 miles [177 km] in 108 hours, and in that time had a three hour's fight. Our regiment lost one man in every five—going in five hundred strong and losing one hundred

killed, wounded and missing. . . . Before going into battle [we] were double-quicked for a mile, and as [we] went in, General Seymour said, "The day is lost; you must go in and save the corps." We did go in and did save it, checked the enemy, held the field, and were the last to leave—and covered the retreat.

By the end of the Civil War, sixteen African-American soldiers had received the nation's highest award, the Congressional Medal of Honor, as had four African-American sailors. But black troops paid a heavy price. There were 68,178 dead or missing in action. Thousands more were wounded.

The end of the Civil War, and the end of slavery, marked a new beginning for American democracy. In the words of Tom Taylor, an African-American Civil War soldier, "The old flag never did wave right. There was something wrong about it. There wasn't any star in it for the black man. . . . But since the war, it's all right. The black man has his star; it is the big one in the middle."

Reconstruction

1865–1877

On April 9, 1865, General Robert E. Lee surrendered to General Ulysses S. Grant at Appomattox Court House in Virginia. The Civil War was over. Although slavery had been abolished, resistance to African-American freedom remained. Four million former slaves, most without skills, land, or money, looked to the U.S. government for help and protection. Anticipating this, Congress had, in March 1865, set up the Freedmen's Bureau under the administration of the U.S. Army.

In the face of tremendous opposition from defeated Confederate supporters, the Freedmen's Bureau attempted to find homes and jobs for former slaves, protect them from unfair labor contracts, and provide them with sufficient food and medicine. The bureau also established forty hospitals and more than four thousand schools, in which approximately 250,000 African-American students eventually enrolled.

Southern state legislatures began to pass a series of laws known as "Black Codes," which limited African-American rights. The codes prevented African-Americans from testifying in court, getting jobs, and enjoying public areas. To counter this discrimination, Pennsylvania congressman Thaddeus

Stevens and Massachusetts senator Charles Sumner got Congress to pass the Reconstruction Act of 1867. It placed ten southern states under military law and established universal male suffrage.

The Fourteenth and Fifteenth Amendments to the U.S. Constitution reinforced the new civil rights legislation. The Fourteenth Amendment states that anyone born in the United States is a citizen and cannot be deprived of "life, liberty or property without due process of law." The Fifteenth Amendment guarantees African-Americans the right to vote. The Thirteenth Amendment, which outlaws slavery, had already been passed.

As a condition for readmission to the Union, all Confederate states had to adopt new state constitutions. Thanks to African-American legislators, such as Blanche K. Bruce and Richard Cain, these new constitutions not only expanded voting rights to African-American men, but also provided free public education and abolished such common criminal punishments as whipping and branding.

Again, former slaveholders fought back. The Ku Klux Klan, a white supremacist organization, sprang up in Tennessee and soon spread throughout the South. Its members beat and murdered thousands of African-Americans who attempted to exercise their civil rights, particularly the right to vote. As a result, U.S. soldiers were stationed at voting booths to protect black voters. In 1877, however, President Rutherford B. Hayes ended the Reconstruction program and withdrew federal troops from the South.

Ku Klux Klan terrorism made many African-Americans afraid to vote. Blacks were pushed out of local and state government, and white legislators passed "Jim Crow" laws that established segregation throughout the South. This situation continued until the Civil Rights Movement of the 1950s and 1960s restored voting rights and ended many types of segregation.

P. B. S. Pinchback

Congressman
1837–1921

One of the most important leaders of the Reconstruction era was Pinckney Benton Stewart Pinchback. The eighth of ten children, he was the son of a white Mississippi planter, William Pinchback, and a former slave of African, Native American, and white ancestry. Shortly before Pinchback's birth in 1837, his mother, Eliza Stewart, and her children were sent to live in Philadelphia. When William died, Eliza Stewart and her children were denied money from his estate. To help support the family, young Pinchback went to work as a cabin boy on canal and Mississippi riverboats.

At the outbreak of the Civil War, Pinchback volunteered for the Union army. He was assigned to recruit African-American soldiers but soon quit in protest over the army's discrimination against them. Taking an aggressive stand, Pinchback demanded political rights for African-Americans, arguing that they should not be drafted if they could not vote. At the conclusion of the war, Pinchback became active in the Republican party in Louisiana. He was a strong supporter of universal suffrage, a free public school system, and guaranteed civil rights for all people.

Elected to the Louisiana State Senate in 1868, Pinchback introduced legislation outlawing racial discrimination in public places. In 1870, he established the *New Orleans Louisianian,* a newspaper that remained in operation for eleven years. In 1871, he became lieutenant governor when Oscar J. Dunn, another African-American legislator, died. Then, when Governor Henry Clay Warmoth was impeached, Pinchback served as acting governor from December 9 to January 13.

In 1872, Pinchback was elected congressman-at-large and also U.S. senator. Both elections were contested, which was not uncommon; several African-Americans elected to Congress were prevented from taking their seats. In a speech that outlined many of his principles, Pinchback defended his election:

> . . . several Senators . . . think me a very bad man. . . . But of what does my badness consist? I am bad because I have dared on several important occasions to have an independent opinion. I am bad because I have dared at all times to advocate and insist on exact and equal justice to all mankind. I am bad because having colored blood in my veins, I have dared to aspire to the United States Senate. . . . I have been told that if I dared utter such sentiments as these in public that I certainly would be kept out of the Senate; all I have to say in answer to this is that if I cannot enter the Senate except with bated breath and on bended knees, I prefer not to enter at all.

Pinchback was never allowed to take his Senate seat. Instead, he was given $16,666 to cover some of the salary he would have received as an active senator. Although he was denied his seat, Congress could not deny Pinchback's importance in the struggle for civil rights.

Booker T. Washington

Educator, Presidential Advisor
1856–1915

*No greater injury can be done to any youth
than to let him feel that because he belongs
to this or that race he will be advanced in life
regardless of his own merits or efforts.*

—Booker T. Washington

When the Civil War ended in 1865, Booker T. Washington was nine years old. He moved to Malden, West Virginia, with his mother, a former slave, and other members of his family. There he went to work as a miner, getting up at 4:00 A.M. to work all day. At night he taught himself to read.

In search of a better education, Washington left home in 1872 to attend Hampton Normal and Agricultural Institute in Virginia. Because he had little money, he was forced to travel most of the way on foot. Once there, he got a job as a janitor to pay for his room and board. A white benefactor paid his tuition. Four years later, Washington graduated with honors and was chosen to speak at his commencement.

In 1881, the Alabama legislature decided to establish a school at Tuskegee to train African-American teachers. Samuel C. Armstrong, head of Hampton Institute, recommended that Washington run the new school, which was housed temporarily in an old church. Determined to make the school successful, Washington borrowed money to purchase an abandoned plantation, where students eventually built classrooms, dormitories, and a chapel and developed skills in farming, carpentry, printing, and shoemaking.

Under Washington's leadership, Tuskegee soon became a leading African-American institution. By 1888, it had a student body of more than 400 and owned 540 acres of land. Washington also attracted many fine African-American teachers to the school, including the great scientist George Washington Carver.

In his efforts to raise money for Tuskegee, Washington became friendly with many of America's leading white businessmen. In 1900, he established the National Negro Business League to encourage the development of African-American-owned businesses. He also wrote his autobiography, *Up from Slavery*, which became a best-seller and was translated into more than a dozen languages. Considered by many to be one of the most important African-American leaders of his time, Washington was asked by Presidents William Howard Taft and Theodore Roosevelt for his advice on several political appointments.

Washington believed African-Americans would advance through hard work, and respect and acceptance by the white community would result. He appeared to accept the existence of segregation while urging whites to support African-American education and economic development. In a major speech in Atlanta, Georgia, he said, "The wisest among the race understand [that seeking] social equality is the extremist folly." This infuriated other African-American leaders, many of whom felt Washington was ignoring the erosion of blacks' political and civil rights in order to promote African-American economic development.

Privately, Washington was more concerned with the increasing threats to African-American rights than his white supporters or black critics realized. He paid the legal fees of several lawyers working to overturn segregation and discriminatory laws. He also used his position to maintain African-American influence in the Republican party in the South.

In spite of the criticism he received from some black leaders, Washington was admired by African-American people throughout the country. He spent his life preaching hard work and perseverance. By practicing what he preached, he turned Tuskegee into a model for other African-American schools and had a major impact on future African-American education. Washington died at Tuskegee in October 1915.

Nat Love

Cowboy
1854—1921

A former slave from Tennessee, his real name was Nat Love, but as a result of a book based on his life, he became known everywhere as Deadwood Dick. He was a gunfighter, scout, range boss, rodeo rider, and—to hear him tell it—the best all-around cowboy in the West. He survived outlaw attacks, capture by Native Americans, and fourteen gun-shot wounds.

Love's adventures began in 1869 when he got lucky and won a horse in a raffle. He sold his horse, split the money with his mother, paid a few bills, and took off for Dodge City, Kansas, to become a cowboy.

Already an experienced horse trainer, Love quickly learned to herd and brand cattle and to use a gun. He got his first job at the Duval ranch. Later, he hired on with the Peter Gallinger outfit.

In 1876, a big Fourth of July celebration was held in Deadwood, South Dakota. The town was crowded with cowboys from all over the territory. It was during this celebration that Love competed in several contests that made him famous. He won the rifle and handgun matches and set a record in the rope throw and bronco-riding contest.

As the West became settled, Love left range life and took a job on the railroad. Like thousands of other African-American men and women who had left behind memories of slavery, he traveled west seeking a fresh start. It is estimated that one-fifth of America's cowboys were African-American men seeking to make a new life for themselves. As pioneers, they played a major part in settling the West and made life easier for thousands of people who came later.

Jan Ernst Matzeliger

Inventor
1852—1889

If the shoe fits, it's partly because a man named Jan Ernst Matzeliger invented a machine that knocked shoe manufacturers right off their feet.

Matzeliger was born in Paramaribo, Suriname (then called Dutch Guiana), in South America. His mother was a black woman from Suriname, and his father was a wealthy Dutch engineer from Holland. At age ten, Matzeliger went to work in a machine shop. When he was nineteen, he got a job on an East Indian merchant ship and spent the next two years at sea. When the ship docked in Philadelphia, he decided to give life in the United States a try.

After working at various jobs in Philadelphia, Matzeliger moved to Boston in 1876 and, a year later, settled in Lynn, Massachusetts, where he got a job with a shoe manufacturing company. Meanwhile, he started night school to study physics and improve his English. In his spare time, he painted and gave art lessons.

As Matzeliger worked in the shoe manufacturing company, he noticed that production was slow because workers had to attach the bottom of the shoe to the top by hand. He decided to invent a machine that could perform this task. Within six months, he had built his first model from wood, wire, and cigar boxes. Although it was far from perfect, it was impressive enough to attract a $50 offer, which he rejected.

In 1880, Matzeliger completed a more advanced model. This one got him a $1,500 offer. Although he needed the money, he turned down the offer again and began work on a third model. He soon realized, however, that he would need financial help. He got it from Melville S. Nichols and Charles H. Delnow, in exchange for a two-thirds interest in his machines.

On March 20, 1883, Matzeliger received patent no. 274,207 for a "Lasting Machine" that would rapidly stitch the leather of a shoe to the sole. Its drawings were so complicated that a scientist from the patent office in Washington, D.C., had to travel to Lynn to observe the machine in action before he could understand it. It was worth the trip. Matzeliger's lasting machine made it possible to turn out 150 to 700 pairs of shoes a day, instead of only 50 pairs a day previously. It also cut manufacturing costs in half.

Anticipating success, Matzeliger, Nichols, and Delnow established the Union Lasting Machine Company and went into business. Soon, they sold out to a larger company. Matzeliger sold all his patents (five by this time) in return for stock in the company.

In 1886, Matzeliger became ill with tuberculosis and died three years later at the age of thirty-seven. He left his stock in the Union Lasting Machine Company to the North Congregational Church, the one church in Lynn that had not rejected him because of his race. As for the company that owned his patents, it became the United Shoe Machine Corporation. Sixty-five years later, it was worth over $1 billion.

Isaac Myers

Labor Leader
1835–1891

Born in Baltimore, Maryland, to free parents, Isaac Myers became an apprentice at age sixteen to James Jackson, an African-American man well known in the ship-caulking business. By age twenty, Myers had been promoted to superintendent and placed in charge of the caulking of clean-line clipper ships.

In 1860, Myers became chief porter and clerk in the Woods, Bridges & Co. grocery business. Four years later, he took over the management of another grocery store. In 1865, he resigned and returned to ship-caulking. That same year white caulkers and ship carpenters went on strike, demanding that all black caulkers and longshoremen be fired. Over a thousand African-American men lost their jobs.

Myers reacted by proposing that the African-American workers band together and buy a shipyard and railway. Within six months, Baltimore African-Americans had raised $10,000, and the project, known as the Chesapeake Marine Railway and Dry Dock Company, was underway. It employed three hundred African-American men at a wage of $3 a day.

Myers also organized a black union known as the Colored Caulkers' Trade Union Society. Myers's organization helped secure African-American caulkers and prevented whites from attempting to drive blacks out of other industries.

In 1871, Myers arranged for what, at that time, was the biggest convention of African-American men in U.S. history. After five days of intense debate, the participants established the Colored National Union, with Myers as president.

In 1879, Myers opened a coal yard, and he later became editor of the *Colored Citizen,* a weekly newspaper. In 1888, he became secretary of the Republican Campaign Committee and organized the Maryland Colored State Industrial Fair Association. Other posts included president of the Colored Businessmen's Association, head of the first Baltimore Building and Loan Association, superintendent of the Bethel A.M.E. School in Baltimore, and a grand master of the Masons. Myers also authored a play, *The Missionary.* But he is best known as a labor leader—and nobody worked harder than he did.

George Jordan

Soldier
1847–1904

On the night of May 13, 1880, George Jordan, an African-American soldier in charge of twenty-five troopers, received word that a small, white settlement located near the Mescalero Indian Reservation in New Mexico was in serious danger of attack. Ordering his men to mount up, Jordan and his group rode through the night to reach the settlement.

Once there, the troopers erected a stockade for the protection of the settlers, positioned themselves for combat, and waited. At sunset, one hundred Apaches attacked. Although they were outnumbered four to one, Jordan and his men drove off the Apaches. Regrouping, the Apaches charged again. Forced back a second time, the Apaches rode off and never returned.

Born in Williamson County, Kentucky, Jordan lived there until 1866, when he enlisted in the newly established Ninth Cavalry. The Ninth Calvary was one of four all-black military units operating in the West. Two of them, the famous Twenty-fourth and Twenty-fifth Regiments, were infantry. The other two, the Ninth and Tenth, were cavalry made up mainly of experienced Civil War veterans, whom Native Americans nicknamed Buffalo Soldiers. Famous for their courage and fighting ability, these

African-American soldiers made up 20 percent of the cavalrymen in the Old West.

In addition to serving in the West, these regiments also saw action during the Spanish-American War (1898). Soldiers from the Ninth and Tenth Cavalry are often credited with saving the day for Theodore Roosevelt's Rough Riders at the Battles of San Juan Hill and Las Guasimas. Said a white officer, "If it had not been for the Negro cavalry, the Rough Riders would have been exterminated. . . . the Negroes saved that fight." Teddy Roosevelt said, "I don't think that any Rough Rider will ever forget the tie that binds us to the Ninth and Tenth Cavalry."

Jordan served faithfully with the army for thirty years and participated in numerous campaigns against Native Americans, Mexican bandits, and American outlaws. He received the Congressional Medal of Honor for the leadership and courage he demonstrated in 1880 when he fought the Apache in New Mexico.

During his last years of active duty, Jordan was stationed at Fort Robinson, Nebraska. Following his retirement, he moved to Crawford, Nebraska, where he became a leader in the African-American community. When he became sick in 1904, Jordan returned to Fort Robinson for medical help. The army doctor refused to treat him, saying there was no room in the hospital. Jordan died a few days later.

Although the army treated Jordan poorly, history does not. Today, Jordan, along with other Buffalo Soldiers, takes his place among America's most courageous fighting men.

Scott Joplin
Composer, Pianist
1868–1917

In the years following the Civil War, scores of African-American musicians traveled throughout the country, playing in churches and saloons and trying to earn enough money to eat. Building on old African rhythms, they developed new musical forms that were uniquely American. One of these musicians, Scott Joplin, became the leading composer of ragtime.

Born in Texarkana, Texas, in 1868, Joplin grew up playing piano in houses where his mother, Florence, worked as a maid. Word of his exceptional talent soon spread throughout the community, and a German music teacher offered to give young Joplin formal training.

Within a short time, Joplin was playing in churches as well as for social events. Shortly after his mother died, he left home to become a professional musician. As he traveled across the country, Joplin was attracted to ragtime, a rapidly growing form of African-American music that had evolved from the old slave songs. Drawing on African traditions, ragtime combined a syncopated, or varied, rhythm pattern with the melody. This technique, known as "ragging" the melody, was especially popular in dance music. Dances were often called rags.

In 1895, Joplin moved to St. Louis and got a job playing piano at "Honest" John Turpin's Silver Dollar Saloon. Several years later he settled in Sedalia, Missouri, where he began to study and write music. During the day,

Joplin took courses in music theory at George R. Smith College. At night, he played piano in the Maple Leaf Club.

In 1899, Scott published "Original Rags," a beautifully crafted work. Later, he took another piece, "Maple Leaf Rag" (named for the club where he worked), to two publishers. Both rejected it. Both made a big mistake. A music dealer named John Stark heard the piece and printed it.

Within a few months, "Maple Leaf Rag" had sold more than 600,000 copies. Considered by many to be the best rag ever written, it became the first piece of sheet music to sell more than a million copies. Its publication brought world-wide demand for ragtime music, which thrived until the end of World War I.

The publication of "Maple Leaf Rag" brought Joplin financial security. It allowed him to quit playing in saloons and concentrate on teaching and writing music. Although none of his later work had the financial success of "Maple Leaf Rag," it was all of excellent quality.

But Joplin wasn't satisfied with putting ragtime on the musical map. He wanted to write opera. His first attempt, *The Guest of Honor,* closed after only a few performances. But it was a work called *Treemonisha,* written partly in tribute to his mother, that meant the most to him. Joplin was determined to see *Treemonisha* performed on stage. Unable to find backers, he decided to produce it himself, but his efforts were in vain. The audience didn't understand or appreciate the opera, and it closed. Joplin was devastated.

In 1916, Joplin was committed to Manhattan State Hospital, where he died the following April. At the time of his death, ragtime was fading in popularity. Young people thought it was old-fashioned and were now more interested in jazz. But Joplin's music was too good to be forgotten. In the 1970s, Joplin's rag "The Entertainer" was chosen as the theme for the Academy Award-winning movie *The Sting,* and his opera *Treemonisha* was dusted off and finally produced on Broadway, where it became a hit. It was a fitting tribute to the man music experts call the "King of Ragtime."

George Washington Williams

Historian, Lawyer, Soldier
1849–1891

George Washington Williams's career started during the Civil War, when he lied about his age (he was fourteen, not eighteen as required) and joined the Sixth Massachusetts Regiment under his uncle's name. The army soon discovered the truth and put him out. Not long afterward, Williams reenlisted and became a sergeant major on the staff of General N. P. Jackson. Fighting in several battles, he was wounded in a skirmish near Fort Harrison, Virginia, in 1864 and was discharged a year later.

Williams then joined the Mexican army. He resigned after about a year and enlisted in the U.S. Tenth Cavalry. This time, he took part in the campaign against the Comanche, was wounded, and received a medical discharge in 1868.

Having had enough of military life, Williams decided to become a minister. He enrolled at the Newton Theological Institution in Massachusetts and graduated in 1874. The following year, he became an ordained minister and served as pastor of the Twelfth Street Church in Boston. After a year, he moved to Washington, D.C., where he started a newspaper called *The Commoner*. Even though the paper had the support of such people as Frederick Douglass, it eventually failed. In 1876, Williams settled in

Cincinnati, where he resumed his ministry at the Union Baptist Church.

Once again, one career was not enough for Williams. Besides becoming a journalist and writing for several newspapers, he began to study law. In 1879, he was admitted to the bar and elected to the Ohio legislature.

Politics did not hold Williams for long either. While continuing to serve as a legislator, he began collecting information on the history of African-American people in the United States. After extensive research, he wrote an impressive two-volume book called *History of the Negro Race in America from 1619 to 1880*. Published in 1882, it became the first extensive work of its kind by an African-American and was an immediate success. Williams's second book, *History of the Negro Troops in the War of Rebellion*, was published in 1888. This, too, was widely praised.

As a result of his successful books, Williams became a popular lecturer and made several trips to Europe. On one of these trips, he met King Leopold II of Belgium, who convinced him to help develop the Congo Free State in Africa. Though it was called a "Free State," the Congo was a colony owned by the king.

Williams decided to visit the place. The trip proved to be a tremendous shock for him. Although Leopold said he was opposed to slavery, Williams found that the Congolese were treated like slaves. Forced to work long hours on the rubber plantations, they were subjected to terrible punishments when they failed to produce enough.

Outraged by what he saw, Williams wrote "An Open Letter to His Serene Majesty, Leopold II, King of the Belgians." In it, he denounced the king and his rule in Africa. The report made a strong impact not only in Belgium but also in the United States, France, and England. An international campaign to end the cruel conditions in the Congo resulted. Williams then followed up with two more reports and an investigation of the Portuguese and British colonies in Africa. He was working on another report on the Congo Free State when he became ill and died in 1891.

George Washington Carver

Scientist, Educator
1861–1943

Education is the key to unlock the golden door of freedom.

—George Washington Carver

Most people just eat peanuts. George Washington Carver developed 325 different products from them, including coffee, face powder, ink, butter, shampoo, vinegar, soap, and wood stains.

Carver was born of slave parents in 1861 on a plantation belonging to Moses and Susan Carver near Diamond, Missouri. When he was just a baby, Carver and his mother were kidnapped and taken to Arkansas. Within a short time, George was returned to the Carver plantation, but his mother was never found. A sickly child, he was unable to do heavy work and, instead, spent much of his time wandering in the nearby woods collecting flowers and plants.

After the Civil War, George and his brother James continued to live on the Carver plantation, where George taught himself to read. At age ten, he left the plantation. For the next few years, he worked at odd jobs and attended school whenever he could. Finally, he enrolled at Minneapolis High School in Kansas and won a scholarship to attend Highland University. When he showed up at Highland, however, the school refused to admit him

George Washington Carver conducts experiments in his laboratory.

because he was black. Carver was not discouraged. He continued to work and save money. Years later, he was accepted at Simpson College in Iowa, where he supported himself by ironing clothes for fellow students.

Although Carver was artistically inclined, he was more interested in science. With the help of his art teacher, he was accepted at Iowa Agricultural College in 1891. His work in botany and chemistry was so outstanding that, upon graduation, he was asked to stay on as an assistant instructor and director of the greenhouse. While teaching, Carver continued his own research. He conducted important investigations into several varieties of fungi that damaged wheat, soybeans, oats, blackberries, and maple trees.

In 1896, Carver received a letter from Booker T. Washington, founder of Tuskegee Institute in Alabama, asking him to work there. Tuskegee was a poor school and could not offer him much in the way of salary or laboratory equipment. Nevertheless, Carver agreed to go.

At Tuskegee, Carver developed a system of crop rotation. He planted legumes (crops such as peanuts, which replenish nitrogen in the soil) one year, followed by cotton the next year. The purpose of rotation was to keep the soil rich and improve the harvest. This system became so successful that an oversupply of peanuts resulted. Carver responded by coming up with more than two dozen uses for the crop. Soon, farmers were making more money raising peanuts than they made harvesting cotton.

While continuing to develop uses for the peanut, Carver began to experiment with the sweet potato. Before long, he had discovered 118 products that could be made from it, including dyes, ink, and synthetic rubber. As his work progressed, he was visited by the crown prince of Sweden and the British Prince of Wales. Thomas Edison asked him to join his staff at a yearly salary of more than $100,000; automobile manufacturer Henry Ford also made a generous offer. Carver preferred to remain at Tuskegee.

Unconcerned about money or material possessions, Carver concentrated on his research, hoping to improve the lives of African-American farmers. "It has always been the one great ideal of my life," he said, "to be of the greatest good to the greatest number of my people."

Carver died in 1943. The George Washington Carver National Monument and museum, located in southwestern Missouri, commemorates this extraordinary man.

Granville T. Woods

Inventor
1856–1910

Known as "The Black Edison," Granville T. Woods was a brilliant inventor of electromechanical devices. He received nearly fifty patents during his lifetime for inventions ranging from a telephone transmitter to an electrically heated egg incubator.

Woods was born in Columbus, Ohio, in 1856. At age ten, he was forced to quit school and go to work. By sixteen, he had moved to Missouri, where he worked as a fireman and an engineer on the railroads. Then he moved to New York City, where he studied electrical engineering while working as an engineer on the British steamship *Ironsides*.

Returning to Ohio in 1884, Woods and his brother Lyates opened a machine shop in Cincinnati and began manufacturing telephone, telegraph, and electrical equipment. The same year, Woods received his first patent for an improved telephone transmitter. The American Bell Telephone Company of Boston quickly bought the rights to it.

In 1885, Woods invented a device that combined features of the telephone and the telegraph. By 1887, he had patented seven more machines, one of which could telegraph messages to moving trains, warning railroad personnel of dangers on the tracks. Over the next fifteen years, Woods patented an amazing array of inventions: electromagnetic brakes, an automatic safety cutoff for electrical circuits, a light dimmer, an overhead conducting system for trolley cars, and an electrified "third rail" that became an important element of subway systems.

Of the forty-five patents credited to Woods, many were sold to such companies as General Electric, Westinghouse, and American Bell Telephone. Unfortunately, he died in poverty, much of his money having been lost to legal fees resulting from a libel suit brought against him when he charged an American Engineering Company manager with stealing patents.

Few scientists can match the genius of Woods. His inventions modernized the transportation systems in the United States and provided a spark that moved the electronics industry forward.

Daniel Hale Williams

Surgeon, Educator
1858–1931

Today, we often speak about heart transplants and artificial hearts. In 1893, people were talking about the world's first successful heart operation and the surgeon who performed it— Daniel Hale Williams.

The patient was a man named James Cornish who had been stabbed in the heart and left for dead. He was brought to Chicago's Provident Hospital where, without the aid of penicillin, antibiotics, or X rays, Williams performed what many believe was a medical miracle. He actually sewed up a torn heart and saved his patient's life.

Born in Hollidaysburg, Pennsylvania, on January 18, 1858, Williams went to work at age twelve as an apprentice to a shoemaker. During the next few years, he worked at various jobs, always hoping he could return to school someday.

Moving to Wisconsin, Williams became an apprentice to Dr. Henry Palmer, who helped him attend Chicago Medical College. Graduating in only three years, Williams set up practice in Chicago and joined the surgical staff at the South Side Dispensary. He also became an instructor at Chicago Medical College and, in 1889, was appointed to the Illinois State Board of Health.

Concerned that there was no hospital for African-Americans in Chicago, Williams established the Provident Hospital and Training Association in 1891. It provided hospital care for all patients, as well as training for African-American physicians and nurses. It was here, in Provident Hospital, that Williams sewed up Cornish's heart.

The operation made news all over the world. When President Grover Cleveland heard about it, he asked Williams to become chief surgeon at Freedman's Hospital in Washington, D.C. Williams accepted and immediately began reorganizing the hospital. He also created a training program for African-American nurses and doctors.

During the Spanish-American War (1898), Williams evaluated and selected surgeons for military service. After the war, he resumed his research and lectured on the need for expanded medical facilities for African-Americans. When he finally retired in 1926, he had helped establish at least forty hospitals serving primarily African-Americans. Physician, scientist, and educator, Williams contributed enormously to the development of surgical theory and practice and greatly expanded medical care and career opportunities for African-Americans.

Madam C. J. Walker

Business Woman, Humanitarian
1867–1919

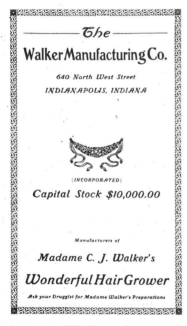

The
Walker Manufacturing Co.

640 North West Street
INDIANAPOLIS, INDIANA

(INCORPORATED)

Capital Stock $10,000.00

Manufacturers of

Madame C. J. Walker's

Wonderful Hair Grower

Ask your Druggist for Madame Walker's Preparations

I am a woman who came from the cotton fields of the South. . . . I promoted myself into the business of manufacturing hair goods and preparations. . . . I have built my own factory on my own ground.

—Madam C. J. Walker

Most people's dreams are forgotten quickly; Madam C. J. Walker turned hers into a million dollars.

Born Sarah Breedlove to former slaves in Louisiana in 1867, Walker was orphaned at age seven. At fourteen, she married a man named McWilliams. Six years later McWilliams died, leaving Walker alone to raise their daughter A'Lelia.

After moving to St. Louis, Missouri, Walker found work as a washerwoman. While working hard to educate her daughter, her hair began to fall out. Although she tried various remedies, nothing seemed to help. Then one night, she dreamed about an old man who showed her things to mix up for her hair. When she awoke, she gave the formula a try. After combining the various ingredients, she tested the mixture on herself. "My hair was coming in faster that it had ever fallen out," she said. "I tried in on my friends; it helped them. I made up my mind that I would sell it."

In July 1905, Walker moved to Denver, Colorado. Six months later, she married a newspaperman named Charles Walker and began calling herself Madam C. J. Walker. She began to travel widely, demonstrating her beauty preparations and, in 1908, opened a second office in Pittsburgh. Walker advertised extensively in African-American newspapers. In 1910, she established her own factory, and a college to train "hair culturists," in Indianapolis. By then her company was earning $7,000 a week.

During this time, African-American women were among the lowest-paid workers in the United States. Victimized by both race and sex discrimination, those not working as sharecroppers or on farms were employed mainly as domestic workers and washerwomen. For the approximately five thousand African-American women working for Walker, there was better pay, greater opportunity, and more dignity. She insisted that "loveliness" was linked to "cleanliness" rather than race. In a society where white skin and Caucasian features were the standard for beauty, Walker's assertion that African-American women were beautiful helped many change their self-image.

Always concerned about the African-American community, Walker organized her women agents into "Walker Clubs" and provided cash prizes for outstanding community service. She contributed generously for scholarships to Tuskegee, to the National Association for the Advancement of Colored People (NAACP), and to other African-American charities in the United States and abroad. She helped direct a fundraising drive to establish Mary McLeod Bethune's school in Daytona and donated the money needed to pay off the mortgage on Frederick Douglass's home. A woman of determination, energy, and vision, Walker became America's first black woman millionaire.

Charles Young

Soldier
1864–1922

I am always willing to aid in any work for the good of the country in general and our race in particular.

—Charles Young

Charles Young was born in a log cabin in Mayslick, Kentucky. The third African-American man to graduate from West Point, he was assigned to Fort Robinson, Nebraska, where he joined the famous Ninth Cavalry. After serving there for four years, he was transferred to Fort Du Chesne, Utah, and was later selected to teach French, mathematics, tactics, and military science at Wilberforce University in Ohio.

When the Spanish-American War began in 1898, Young was placed in command of the Ninth Ohio Volunteer Infantry and sent to Cuba. In 1901, he was transferred to the Philippines, where his men nicknamed him "Follow Me" because of his courage and leadership.

Because of his distinguished military record, Young was made military attaché to Haiti in 1904. While serving as attaché, he explored Haiti and the Dominican Republic and sent back lengthy reports on the island and its people. He also made detailed maps of previously uncharted areas. Young's diplomatic accomplishments were due in part to his interest in different people and cultures, and to his readiness to learn. He spoke Latin, Greek,

German, French, Spanish, and Italian; played the piano and the violin; and composed poetry. While in Haiti, Young wrote a book called *Military Morale of Nations of Races,* an English-French-Creole dictionary, and a play.

Young was assigned as military attaché to Liberia in 1912. As he had done previously in Haiti, he charted maps of the country and studied the native culture. It was often dangerous work. One time, while on a mission to rescue an American officer who had been ambushed by Gola tribesmen, he was shot and wounded in the right arm.

After returning from Liberia, Young served with General John J. Pershing in Mexico. He established a school for African-American enlisted men at Fort Huachucha, hoping many of them would later be able to qualify for officer's training.

At the outbreak of World War I, Colonel Young looked forward to commanding African-American troops in Europe. He was denied a command, however, when Army doctors diagnosed him as suffering from high blood pressure and an advanced case of nephritis (Bright's disease). Believing the denial of command was racially motivated, Young rode his horse 497 miles (800 km) from Ohio to Washington, D.C., to prove he was fit for combat. It didn't help. Though he protested bitterly, he was forced to retire from active duty on June 22, 1917. However, in 1919, the State Department asked him to return to Africa as a military attaché and special advisor to the Liberian government. Three years later, on January 8, 1922, Young died of nephritis while on a visit to Lagos, Nigeria.

Colonel Young served in the army at a time when African-American men were generally thought unfit to be high-ranking officers. The nine black men appointed to West Point before him had faced tremendous hostility and prejudice. In the face of such opposition, Young's accomplishments were amazing indeed.

Elijah McCoy

Inventor

1843–1929

When Elijah McCoy's parents escaped from slavery in Kentucky via the Underground Railroad, they did not anticipate having a son whose inventions would affect railroad transportation all over the world.

Born in Ontario, Canada, in 1843, McCoy was the third of twelve children. After attending school near his home, he went to Edinburgh, Scotland, where he studied mechanical engineering. Moving to Detroit to find work, McCoy was forced to take a job as a fireman on the Michigan Central Railroad, where prejudice kept him from being hired as an engineer.

In those days, trains and other machinery were stopped every day to be oiled. Recognizing this as a great waste of time and money, McCoy started the Elijah McCoy Manufacturing Company and developed a device that would lubricate machinery automatically while it was still in operation. In 1872, he received a patent for his steam-engine lubricator, the "lubricator cup." McCoy kept improving his device and developed variations of it. In time, he received forty-two patents for his inventions, which saved millions of dollars. Soon his systems were in use all over the world.

Although others tried to copy his work, people continued to demand the original. Using a phrase that has now become part of the American language, people said they wanted the "Real McCoy."

Henry Ossawa Tanner

Artist
1859–1937

Born in 1859, Henry Ossawa Tanner was given his middle name because his father, an African Methodist Episcopal minister, admired John Brown, who had killed five pro-slavery settlers near the Osawatomie settlement in Kansas three years earlier.

Tanner began painting at an early age. In 1879, he entered the Pennsylvania Academy of Fine Arts. There he met artist and teacher Thomas Eakins, who greatly influenced his work. Although Tanner had the support of Eakins and the other instructors, many students were jealous of his work and angry that an African-American would aspire to a career as an artist. One night, they tied him to his easel and dumped him in the middle of Broad Street. After two years of this kind of treatment, Tanner left the academy. Some critics think Tanner's painting, *The Battle of Life*, which pictures an elk being attacked by wolves, was really Tanner's artistic way of expressing the attacks he had suffered.

After several years of financial struggle, Tanner took a job teaching at Clark University in Atlanta. Then, in 1891, he left for Europe. Arriving in Paris, Tanner enrolled at the Académie Julian, where he became the favorite pupil of artist Jean-Joseph Benjamin-Constant. Tanner loved living in France, but after a bout with typhoid fever, he returned home to recover. He continued to paint and completed one of his most famous pictures, *The Banjo Lesson.*

Known for his many paintings on biblical themes, Tanner traveled to Egypt and what is now Israel to work. The brutality of World War I shocked Tanner, who developed a gardening program for wounded soldiers in France. The program was so successful that in 1923, the French government awarded him the Legion of Honor. Today Tanner is regarded as one of America's most talented artists.

Ida B. Wells-Barnett

Journalist, Civil Rights Activist
1862–1931

Christian and moral forces . . . should insist that . . . this nation do its duty to exalt justice and preserve inviolate the sacredness of human life.

—Ida B. Wells-Barnett

It was called "A Red Record"—the first complete list of lynchings in the United States during a three-year period—and the bloody title fit. In the ten years from 1890 to 1900, 1,217 African-Americans were murdered by lynch mobs. Compiled by Ida Wells-Barnett in 1895, this report set the tone for her lifelong crusade against lynching.

Born a slave in Holly Springs, Mississippi, Ida Wells struggled to gain an education. When she was sixteen, her parents died within a day of each other. Lying about her age, Wells became a teacher. She was the sole supporter of five brothers and sisters. Her pay was $25 a month.

In 1884, Wells moved to Memphis, where she continued to teach. When she complained of poor conditions in the school, however, she was fired. In the meantime, she had begun writing for the *Living Way* newspaper. With a little money she had managed to save, she bought an interest in the

Memphis *Free Speech and Headlight,* which also published her work. Within nine months, subscriptions to the *Free Speech* had increased by two thousand. Threats against her life also increased.

Nonetheless, when three African-American men were dragged from jail in 1892 and lynched, Wells did more than complain. She named the men who were directly involved and the city officials who refused to take action. She also wrote articles urging African-Americans to boycott the new streetcar line and, if possible, to leave the city entirely. Within two months, approximately two thousand African-Americans had moved away, and the streetcar company was almost bankrupt.

At the time, many people accepted lynching as a satisfactory way of punishing African-American criminals, but Wells knew that the men who were lynched in Memphis were not criminals. They had been killed because they had set up a successful grocery store that was taking business away from a competing white-owned store. If the men hanged in Memphis had been innocent, thought Wells, then many other lynch victims might have been innocent as well.

Determined to uncover the truth, she began traveling across the country, interviewing eyewitnesses and visiting the scenes of various lynchings. Of the 728 murders she investigated, she found that only one-third involved African-Americans actually accused of crimes, let alone convicted of them. Most lynch victims were murdered for "quarreling with whites," for "making threats," or because of "race prejudice." Not only men, but also women and children, had been murdered by mobs.

Wells continued to write editorials attacking those who offered excuses for lynch mobs. One day she went a little too far, and an angry mob retaliated by burning her newspaper office. Luckily, she was out of town when it happened, and she knew she would have to leave Memphis for her own safety. Moving to New York, she continued to make herself heard.

On June 5, 1892, the *New York Age* carried a long article written by Wells. In it, she revealed the names, dates, places, and brutal details of hundreds of lynchings. Ten thousand copies of the paper were sold, including a thousand in Memphis alone. In addition to writing, Wells traveled to England to gain support for her anti-lynching campaign.

In 1895, Wells married lawyer and editor Ferdinand Lee Barnett. With his support, she organized women's clubs and political groups committed to helping African-Americans. Her work in stressing the need for a national African-American organization was instrumental in the founding of the National Association for the Advancement of Colored People (NAACP) in 1909.

In her unceasing struggle to outlaw lynching, Wells-Barnett faced the difficult and often dangerous task of trying to change people's thinking as well as their behavior. Because of her efforts, lynching is now regarded as a vicious crime that no decent person can ignore, justify, or excuse.

Mary Church Terrell

Civil Rights Activist, Educator
1863–1954

The same murders that started Ida Wells-Barnett on her anti-lynching crusade triggered a change in the life of Mary Church Terrell. One of the murder victims had been her close friend. When Terrell heard the news, she called on Frederick Douglass to help arrange a meeting with President Benjamin Harrison. Together, Terrell and Douglass pleaded with Harrison to condemn lynching in his annual message to Congress. When he refused, Terrell took it upon herself to begin a lifelong struggle to wipe out lynching, racism, and sexism.

Terrell was the daughter of Robert Church, a former slave whose extensive real-estate investments had made him the first African-American millionaire in Memphis. In 1884, she graduated from Oberlin College in Ohio; she went on to get her advanced degree in 1888. Much to the displeasure of her father, who thought women should not work, Terrell became an instructor at Wilberforce University. "He disinherited me," said Terrell, "because I went to Wilberforce to teach. I was told that no man would want to marry a woman who studied higher mathematics. I said I'd take a chance." As it turned out, in 1891, she married Robert Terrell, who later became the first African-American judge in the municipal court of the District of Columbia.

In 1895, Terrell was appointed to the board of education in Washington, D.C., becoming the first African-American woman in the country to hold such a position. In spite of her personal success, Terrell faced an uphill battle because many people felt women were intellectually and emotionally inferior to men.

Terrell worked closely with white suffragette leaders Susan B. Anthony and Jane Addams. They were campaigning to win passage of the Nineteenth Amendment to the Constitution, which would give women the right to vote. It was a rocky alliance. The white suffrage groups were often quick to ignore or deny African-Americans' rights if they felt that fighting for blacks would cost them support, especially in the South.

The entry of the United States into World War I in 1917 had a major impact on African-American women. As many whites entered the Army or found better-paying jobs in defense industries, thousands of blacks moved north to take their place. Although the pay was better in the North, blacks generally did not have the protection of the largely white organized labor movement. To improve working conditions and obtain equal treatment for African-American women, Terrell helped form the Women Wage-Earners Association. It organized African-American domestic workers, waitresses, nurses, and tobacco stemmers. She also helped establish the National Association of Colored Women (NACW) and was a founder of the NAACP.

Terrell remained active all her life. At age eighty-six, she began a three-year battle against the American Association of University Women because they refused to admit African-American women. She also led an economic boycott of Washington, D.C., department stores that refused to serve African-Americans. Even at age ninety, she was marching at the head of a picket line to end segregation in restaurants.

Terrell demanded respect not only for herself but also for African-American women everywhere. At a time when women as a group were treated with condescension, and African-American women with contempt, Terrell's was one of the few voices raised on their behalf.

Matthew Alexander Henson

Explorer
1866–1955

Great ideals are the glory of man alone. Only man can get a vision and an inspiration that will lift him above the level of himself and send him forth against all opposition . . . to do and to dare and to accomplish wonderful and great things for the world and for humanity.

—Matthew Alexander Henson

Born in Charles County, Maryland, Matthew Alexander Henson lost his mother when he was only two years old. Six years later, his father died. For a while, Henson attended school in Washington, D.C., where he lived with an uncle. Around the age of twelve, he ran away to Baltimore and signed on as a cabin boy on the merchant ship *Katie Hines*. The ship's commander, Captain Childs, took a liking to the boy, and Henson spent the next six years sailing around the world with him. By the time Henson was eighteen, he had traveled across the Atlantic and Pacific Oceans, the China and Baltic Seas, and through the Straits of Magellan at the tip of South America.

Returning to Washington, D.C., Henson got a job in a clothing store as a clerk. One day in 1887, a naval officer, Robert E. Peary, entered the store.

He said he was planning an expedition to explore building a canal through Nicaragua that would link the Atlantic and Pacific Oceans.

Impressed with Henson, Peary hired him. Henson's seagoing experience and ability to chart a path through jungle terrain made him a valuable associate. The Nicaragua expedition marked the beginning of an association between the two men that would last for more than twenty years.

Peary wanted to be the first man to reach the North Pole, a dream Henson soon came to share. Henson learned to speak the Inuit language and became skilled in making sleds and other equipment needed in the regions of the far north. Together, he and Peary made seven trips to the Arctic. Six times, ice, storms, and subzero temperatures forced them to turn back.

In 1908, they set out on their final expedition. Peary was accompanied by several other white assistants and Inuit guides. Henson was assigned to lead the first dog sled. "He is a better dog driver," said Peary, "and can handle a sledge better than any man living except some of the best Eskimo [Inuit] hunters. I couldn't get along without him."

Six dog teams left Crane City, Greenland, at the edge of the Arctic Circle, established camps, and left supplies. One by one, they returned to Cape Columbia on Canada's Ellesmere Island, where they reunited for the final trek of their 478-mile (769-km) journey to the North Pole.

Travel was often unbearable. Temperatures dropped as low as 60 degrees Fahrenheit (15.6 degrees Celsius) below zero. According to Henson, "We [traveled] eighteen to twenty hours out of every twenty-four. . . . Forced marches all the time [because] we couldn't carry food for more than fifty days, fifty-five at a pinch." Henson moved out in front, his dog team covering 35 miles (56 km) on the first day. Peary followed, moving more slowly because he had had several toes amputated nine years earlier because of frostbite.

On the morning of April 6, 1909, Henson reached 90 degrees north latitude—the North Pole. With the help of two Inuit assistants, Henson built an igloo and waited for Commander Peary to arrive and confirm his calculations. After Peary arrived, the crew spent about 30 hours making observations and taking soundings before planting an American flag and packing up their gear for the long, freezing trip home.

When Henson returned from the expedition, he was so thin his wife didn't even recognize him. Few people were willing to recognize his achievements, either. Not until thirty-six years later was he awarded the Congressional Medal of Honor. Six years after Henson's death in 1955, the State House of Annapolis, Maryland, finally created a commemorative plaque honoring him as codiscoverer of the North Pole.

Mary McLeod Bethune

Educator, Civil Rights Activist
1875–1955

In 1904, Mary McLeod Bethune left home with $1.50 in her pocket and a dream of establishing a school for African-American children. A few months later, she made a down payment on a former garbage dump in Daytona, Florida, where she set up the Daytona Normal and Industrial School. Tuition was fifty cents a week, and the student body consisted of five girls and Mrs. Bethune's son, Albert. Within two years, there were 250 students at what would later become Bethune-Cookman College.

Born in a small cabin near Mayesville, South Carolina, Mary McLeod was the fifteenth of seventeen children. She spent her childhood picking cotton and washing and ironing clothes. For 6 years she walked 5 miles (8 km) to and from school each day. At night, she taught her brothers and sisters what she had learned.

Mary studied hard. She won a scholarship to Scotia Seminary in Concord, North Carolina, and later went to the Moody Bible Institute in Chicago. Graduating in 1895, she became a teacher. Two years later, she married Albertus Bethune. Back then, whites often called black women by their first names as a sign of disrespect, but Mrs. Bethune insisted on being addressed properly.

Mrs. Bethune organized concerts and wrote articles to raise money for her new school. She rode her bicycle to churches, clubs, and organizations, asking for contributions. One day she asked a wealthy businessman, James M. Gamble of Procter & Gamble, for support. When he visited the small shack that was her classroom, he was shocked. "Where is the school?" he asked. "It is in my mind and in my soul," Mrs. Bethune replied. Gamble was so impressed by her reply that he donated $150.

In 1935, Mrs. Bethune founded the National Council of Negro Women to work for the rights and opportunities of African-Americans, especially women. That same year, President Franklin Roosevelt appointed her as a special consultant to the National Youth Administration (NYA), whose purpose was to provide employment and job training for youth. Later, as director of the Negro Division of the NYA, she helped increase educational aid for African-American students. Mrs. Bethune also used her influence to secure a $500,000 grant for an African-American housing project in Daytona and force Johns Hopkins Hospital in Baltimore to hire African-American physicians.

Although Mrs. Bethune's main concerns were the elimination of racial prejudice, improved status of African-American women, and greater job and educational opportunities for African-American youth, she sought to help other persecuted groups as well. When Nazi Germany passed the Nuremberg Laws in 1935, legalizing and extending discrimination against Jews, Mrs. Bethune and the National Council of Negro Women petitioned President Roosevelt to take action on behalf of Jewish victims. Mrs. Bethune became a friend of Theodore Roosevelt and an advisor to five other presidents.

Mrs. Bethune died at age eighty. Her will read, "I leave you love. . . . I leave you hope. . . . I leave you a thirst for education. . . . I leave you a responsibility to our young people." But Mrs. Bethune left more than that. For thousands of African-Americans, especially women and children, she left increased opportunity, dignity, and self-respect.

W. E. B. Du Bois

Civil Rights Leader, Anthropologist, Educator
1868–1963

I believe in the Negro Race: in the beauty of its genius, the sweetness of its soul, and its strength in that meekness which shall yet inherit this turbulent earth.

—W. E. B. Du Bois

A suspicious police agent once asked W. E. B. Du Bois just what the NAACP was fighting for. "For the enforcement of the Constitution of the United States," Du Bois replied.

Born in Great Barrington, Massachusetts, William Edward Burghardt Du Bois was of African, French, and Dutch ancestry. After graduating from high school at age fifteen, he entered Fisk University in Nashville, Tennessee. From there he went to Harvard University, where he received a Ph.D. in 1895. Du Bois then became a professor of English, German, Latin, and Greek at Wilberforce University in Ohio and the University of Pennsylvania.

At the University of Pennsylvania, Du Bois wrote *The Philadelphia Negro*. As a result of this work, he was invited to teach history and economics at Atlanta University. There he directed the Atlanta Studies Program, which published thirteen important studies of African-American life.

Beginning in 1900, Du Bois participated in a series of Pan African conferences, where he demanded independence and self-government for African countries. It was at the first of these conferences in London that Du Bois made his famous prediction, "The problem of the twentieth century is the problem of the color line." He was referring not only to the ongoing civil rights struggle in the United States, but also to efforts to end oppressive European colonial regimes that existed throughout Africa and Asia.

In 1903, Du Bois published his best-known work, a book of essays called *The Souls of Black Folk*. According to James Weldon Johnson, this work "had a greater effect upon and within the black race in America than any other book published in this country since *Uncle Tom's Cabin.*"

Two years later, Du Bois organized the Niagara Movement. Named for the location of its first meeting (near Niagara Falls), the Niagara Movement was set up to demand "full manhood rights" for African-Americans. The movement was the forerunner of the NAACP, which grew out of an anti-lynching conference held in 1909 by a group of black and white leaders.

In 1910, Du Bois established the *Crisis*, the official magazine of the NAACP. Largely because of his writings in the magazine, the NAACP grew rapidly. By 1916, it had sixty-seven branches and nine thousand members.

Du Bois criticized fellow African-American leader Booker T. Washington for his policy of publicly ignoring injustices toward black people for the purpose of maintaining good relations with white people. Du Bois felt African-Americans should fight to protect their Constitutional rights. He believed college-educated African-Americans, who constituted what he called "The Talented Tenth," should take the lead in helping the African-American race to advance.

Leaving the NAACP in 1934, Du Bois returned to Atlanta University. While there, he wrote hundreds of articles and essays. He also published several books, among them the brilliant *Black Reconstruction in America* (1935). Frustrated by the U.S. government's inability to solve the problem of racial discrimination, Du Bois embraced socialism. He became associated with the peace movement and advocated banning nuclear weapons. Because of this, the U.S. government indicted him as a foreign agent in 1951. When he appeared before the judge at his arraignment, the eighty-two-year-old Du Bois stated,

> It is a sad commentary that we must enter a courtroom today to plead Not Guilty to something that cannot be a crime—advocating peace and friendship between the American people and the peoples of the world. . . . In a world which has barely emerged from the horrors of the Second World War, and which trembles on the brink of atomic catastrophe, can it be criminal to hope and work for peace?

Certainly the government thought so, even though protests and statements supporting Du Bois poured in from all over the world. But Judge James McGuire did not, and he threw out the case on November 20, 1951.

Many individuals and organizations turned away from Du Bois after his indictment and refused to publish his writings or hire him as a speaker. The State Department would not allow him to travel outside the country until 1958, and his mail was watched strictly. According to Du Bois, "It was a bitter experience, and I bowed before the storm, but I did not break."

In 1961, at the age of ninety-three, Du Bois joined the Communist Party. Two years later, he gave up his U.S. citizenship and became a citizen of Ghana, where he died on August 27, 1963.

Although Du Bois rejected the United States at the end of his life, his influences here endures. A gifted social scientist, scholar, writer, and advocate of human rights both at home and abroad, he set a standard of leadership that few others have been able to achieve.

Robert Sengstacke Abbott

Newspaper Publisher, Civil Rights Advocate
1870–1940

On May 6, 1905, Robert Sengstacke Abbott took all the money he had—25¢—and founded what would one day become one of the largest and most influential African-American newspapers, the *Chicago Defender*.

After graduating from Kent Law School, Abbott was unsuccessful in establishing a legal practice in Chicago. Fortunately, he had learned the printing trade at his stepfather's newspaper. Realizing he could better fight injustice if he had greater influence, Abbott began his own newspaper. His office consisted of a chair and a card table in the kitchen of his rooming house. His first issue ran 4 pages, and he sold 300 copies door-to-door for 2¢ a copy.

The price was low, but the time was right. Most newspapers ignored the African-American community except when reporting crime. Advocating economic, social, and political justice was usually left to the few African-American papers, which provided an outlet for African-American ideas and writing.

During World War I (1914–18), many African-Americans left the South in search of better jobs and greater freedom in the North. The *Chicago Defender* took the lead in encouraging this "Great Migration," much to the anger of southern whites who feared the loss of cheap labor. Alarmed by the increasing number of lynchings, Abbott printed the following militant slogan in the *Defender:* "If you must die, take at least one with you." The white community was outraged. Many southern towns outlawed the *Defender.* Copies of the paper had to be smuggled into African-American communities; some people caught reading it were beaten.

The *Defender* strongly supported the demands of the NAACP, which were listed in the masthead of the newspaper:

> First we want full manhood suffrage and we want it now. Second, we want discrimination in public accommodations to cease. Third, we claim the right of freemen to walk, talk, and be with them that wish to be with us. Fourth, we want the laws enforced against the rich as well as poor, against capitalist as well as laborer, against white and black. Fifth, we want our children educated. They have a right to know, to think, to aspire. We do not believe in violence. Our enemies, triumphant for the present, are fighting the stars in their courses. Justice and humanity must prevail. We are men, we will be treated as men. And we shall win.

In spite of his militant tone, Abbott tried to ease tensions between the black and white communities. He served on the Chicago Commission of Race Relations and was active in the fight to break down segregated housing patterns. He backed political candidates who were sympathetic to African-American interests and fought to ensure that black workers were included in President Franklin Roosevelt's New Deal labor programs.

After years of effort, Abbott succeeded in making the *Chicago Defender* one of the most important African-American newspapers in the country. It had been a hard, lonely fight. "My friends made fun of me," Abbott said. "They thought it was foolish of me to anticipate success in a field in which so many men before me had failed . . . but I went on fighting the opposition of my adversaries and the indifference of my friends; I emerged victorious."

Garrett Augustus Morgan

Inventor
1875–1963

On July 25, 1916, more than thirty men employed by the Cleveland Waterworks Company were at work in Tunnel No. 5, about 250 feet (76 m) below Lake Erie. Suddenly, a violent explosion ripped through the area, trapping the men and filling the air with deadly gases. Rescue workers immediately arrived on the scene, but the dense smoke prevented them from entering the tunnel. As each minute passed, the chances of reaching the victims alive became more remote.

Then, someone remembered that a man named Garrett Morgan had been demonstrating a new "breathing device," or gas mask, and they contacted him. Earlier, Morgan's invention had won a grand prize at a New York Safety and Sanitation Fair. No one had been too interested in his device then—but they were interested now!

As soon as Morgan was contacted, he and his brother, Frank, rushed to the tunnel entrance. Along with two other volunteers, they put on masks and entered the gas-filled tunnel. Feeling their way in the dark, they searched for the trapped workers. At the entrance to the tunnel, relatives and city officials waited. Would the gas masks work? Would their twenty-minute air supply be enough? What if there were another explosion?

Ten minutes later, Morgan and the volunteers appeared carrying the bodies of unconscious workers. Their work had just begun. Returning to the tunnel again and again, they brought thirty-two workers to safety.

Morgan's rescue mission made news nationwide. Suddenly, every fire department in the country wanted Garrett Morgan's gas mask. Orders poured in. Everyone was interested—until they found out that Morgan was African-American. Then business declined. When Morgan promoted his invention in the South, he was forced to have a white man demonstrate how it worked while he pretended to be a Native American assistant.

Still, Morgan continued to perfect his device. In 1917, the United States entered World War I. Thousands of American soldiers used his gas mask to protect themselves from the enemy's deadly chlorine gas.

Morgan was born on a farm in Paris, Kentucky. He left home at fourteen and moved to Cincinnati, Ohio, where he got a job as a handyman. Because he had had only six years of schooling, he hired a tutor to help him with his grammar. In 1895, he moved again—this time to Cleveland, where he got a job as a sewing machine adjuster. Before long, Morgan had his own sewing machine repair business and, eventually, opened a tailor shop with thirty-two employees.

In 1913, while working with a polish for sewing machine needles, Morgan discovered a process that could straighten hair. Realizing the discovery could make him rich, he established the Morgan Hair Refining Company. He soon became wealthy. It is said Morgan was the first African-American man in Cleveland to own his own car. The car inspired another of Morgan's inventions—the three-way traffic light. It was so successful that he sold the rights to the General Electric Company for $40,000.

Concerned about how poorly African-Americans were being treated, Morgan founded the *Cleveland Call* newspaper to improve coverage of African-American affairs. In 1963, the man whose gas mask had given the breath of life to thousands of people died. He was eighty-eight.

William Christopher Handy

Musician, Composer
1873–1958

When William Christopher Handy was a young boy in Florence, Alabama, his mother told him that his big ears meant he had musical ability. Apparently, she was right. But Handy did not need his mother to tell him that—he knew it already.

As a child, Handy made music with harmonicas, broom handles, combs, earthenware jugs, even a nail that he used like a drumstick against the jawbone of a dead horse. When he was older, he traveled across the country playing with small bands. Life was very hard on the road, and racial prejudice was widespread. Some say when Handy wrote the words, "I hate to see the evening sun go down," he was really thinking of his years on the road and the many small towns where a strange African-American man was not welcome after dark.

Handy's first big hit was "Memphis Blues," written in 1912. It started as a campaign song for Edward "Boss" Crump, the mayor of Memphis, and its popularity soon spread. Although Handy was cheated out of the profits on "Memphis Blues," he went on to write the even more famous "St. Louis

Blues" in 1914 and "Beale Street Blues" in 1917.

When World War I created a labor shortage, many poor African-Americans left the South hoping to find better paying jobs in northern factories. African-American news-papers, particularly the *Chicago Defender,* encouraged this trend. As he traveled from town to town, Handy secretly distributed copies of the *Defender* to local black leaders. This was very dangerous; more than one African-American man was lynched for distributing similar northern "propaganda."

During his travels, Handy began writing down the songs he

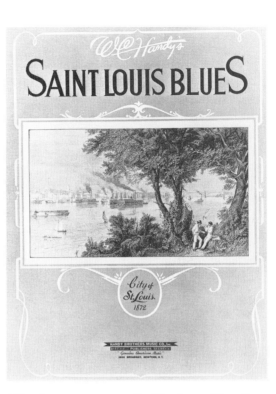

The sheet music cover for "St. Louis Blues"

heard. In 1918, he and his partner, Harry Pace, established the Pace and Handy Music Company. At that time, blues and jazz were becoming popular, and the company was a success. Many of Handy's compositions—"Aunt Hagar's Blues," "A Good Man is Hard to Find," and "Careless Love"— became hits.

Prior to this time, blues was considered the music of poor, ignorant blacks. Handy was determined to change this attitude. Even though he was troubled by serious eye problems and, in 1943, became blind, he continued to write and publish the music of black America. Long ignored by white musicians, blues is now at the forefront of American music, thanks to Handy, the "Father of the Blues."

Henry Johnson

World War I Hero

1897–1929

On April 6, 1917, the United States entered World War I. Approximately ten thousand African-American men had already enlisted in the U.S. Army, and thousands of others were soon signed up. Among the new recruits was a young man from Albany, New York, named Henry Johnson.

Johnson was sent to Camp Wadsworth, South Carolina, for training and assigned to the all-black 369th Infantry. Shortly afterwards, the 369th was shipped out to France, where it was attached to the Sixteenth Division of the French army and sent into action.

On the morning of May 14, 1917, Sergeant Johnson and Private Needham Roberts were on guard duty on a bridge near the Aisne River. Suddenly, without warning, about thirty German soldiers attacked them. Cut off from the other American troops, Johnson and Roberts fought bravely. Wounded and out of ammunition, the two fought on in hand-to-hand combat. When the Germans took Roberts prisoner, Johnson, using only a knife and the butt of his empty rifle, freed him.

Finally, the Germans retreated, but only after Johnson and Roberts had killed at least four of them and wounded about ten others. Afterward,

Johnson and Roberts were taken to a French hospital. Johnson was treated for bayonet and grenade wounds to his back, arm, face, and feet.

The courageous stand these two men had taken had prevented their regiment from suffering heavy casualties. The fight became known as "The Battle of Henry Johnson," and both men were awarded the Croix de Guerre, France's highest military honor.

The 369th Infantry was cited for bravery eleven times during the war. Germans called the African-American infantry unit "Hellfighters" because it never retreated and never allowed one of its members to be captured. But the Hellfighters paid a heavy price. In 191 days of fighting, the 369th suffered 1,500 dead and wounded. Almost 200 of its officers and enlisted men received individual honors; the entire regiment received the Croix de Guerre for gallantry under fire.

When the war ended, the 369th was greeted with a tremendous parade up New York City's Fifth Avenue. Johnson received numerous promises of gifts and honors. The gifts never materialized and, although France had awarded him the highest military honor, he never received even a Purple Heart from the U.S. government. Neither did Johnson receive disability pay, even though he was incapacitated by his wounds and unable to work.

The courage and sacrifice of African-American soldiers in World War I were little appreciated by either the U.S. military or the civilian population. African-American soldiers continued to be segregated in the army and were discriminated against when they tried to find jobs after leaving the service. President Woodrow Wilson had said that the purpose of World War I was to "Make the World Safe for Democracy." Thanks to the sacrifices of men like Johnson, democracy remained safe in most European countries. Unfortunately, the struggle to make President Wilson's slogan a reality at home was far from over.

Bessie Smith

Blues Singer
1894–1937

She once lost a job when she interrupted a song to yell, "Hold on. Let me spit!" That was Bessie Smith, later known to the world as the "Empress of the Blues."

Born in Chattanooga, Tennessee, in 1894, Smith was one of seven children. She grew up poor, and she grew up tough. Both her parents died when she was very young, so she was raised by her older sister Viola.

Smith loved music. When she was only nine years old, she began singing on street corners for nickels and dimes. When she was eighteen, she got a job in a show where she met the great Gertrude "Ma" Rainey, a well-known blues singer who quickly spotted her talent.

For the next few years, Smith traveled from town to town singing in clubs, tents, and theaters. It was a rough life. Often, singers had to work several shows a day in hot, crowded conditions, and theater owners didn't always pay what they had promised. Segregation was the rule throughout the South, and that meant travel was difficult and uncomfortable. Once, a group of Ku Klux Klansmen began to cause trouble. Smith threatened them, saying, "You better pick up them sheets and run!" As she cursed them, they left in a hurry.

By 1920, Smith had become one of the most popular and highest-paid blues singers in the country, attracting black and white audiences alike. She worked with many of the best jazz musicians in the business, including Louis Armstrong, Charlie Green, James P. Johnson, Jack Teagarden, and Benny Goodman. Her singing influenced later artists such as Mahalia Jackson and Billie Holiday.

In 1923, Smith cut her first record, *Down Hearted Blues*. An instant hit, it sold more than two million copies. In fact, the success of Smith's albums kept Columbia Records from going out of business.

Although she earned a lot of money, Smith never forgot the poverty of her early years. This is evident in the lyrics of "Poor Man's Blues":

> Mister rich man, rich man, open up your heart and mind,
> Mister rich man, rich man, open up your heart and mind,
> Give the poor man a chance, help stop these hard, hard times.

For Smith, the "hard times" got even harder when the depression of 1929 hit. Kind and generous, she had given a lot of her money away and had spent much of the rest. Although she was still able to work, the big money was no longer available. Radio was becoming popular and, because of the depression, people were not buying as many records. So Smith began touring the country again with a new show.

Things were going well until Smith was critically injured in an automobile accident near Clarksdale, Mississippi. She died in the Negro Hospital in Clarksdale a short time later.

The Great Northern Migration

Until the early 1900s, most African-Americans lived in the South. Many were the descendants of slaves, and they supported themselves through sharecropping. In 1879, prejudice and Ku Klux Klan violence caused a few thousand of these people, known as Exodusters, to move to Kansas in search of a better life. (The word "Exodusters," which comes from the Biblical book of Exodus, means "leave" or "go out," as the ancient Israelites were led out of Egypt by Moses. The word "exit" also comes from this.)

In the early twentieth century, things began to change. An economic depression from 1913 to 1915 caused cotton prices to fall, creating much hardship. This was made worse by an infestation of boll weevils that destroyed much of the crop. And in Mississippi, in 1915, severe floods destroyed homes and crops.

At the same time, Europe was engaged in World War I (1914–18). Even though the United States did not enter the war until 1917, the conflict kept millions of people from emigrating to America and caused serious labor shortages in northern factories. Black-owned newspapers like the *Chicago*

Defender were quick to point out that a black person in the South who had been earning 50 cents a day could move to New York, Chicago, or Detroit and earn $5 a day.

When the word got out, it didn't take long before hundreds of thousands of African-Americans began packing up and moving north. They found not only better pay, but also less prejudice and more political and educational opportunity. When the South saw that it was in danger of losing its labor force, people tried to prevent the blacks from leaving. In many areas the *Chicago Defender* was banned, but African-American people left anyway. When World War I ended, prejudiced whites in the North attempted to force blacks out of their new jobs. There was violence and rioting, especially during the summer of 1919. But the African-Americans, especially the black soldiers returning from the war, refused to return to the old ways.

The Great Depression of the 1930s threw thousands of people out of work and forced many northern factories to close. As a result, the migration of black people slowed down. But it expanded again during World War II (1941–45), when thousands of men were shipped overseas to fight, and factory owners were desperate for workers. The movement of hundreds of thousands of African-Americans changed the racial composition of hundreds of cities, stimulated black artists and writers, and gave black people much more political power. It was a good move all around.

James Weldon Johnson

Writer, Songwriter, Civil Rights Leader, Diplomat
1871–1938

James Weldon Johnson was born in Jacksonville, Florida, and went to Atlanta University in Georgia. In 1895, he founded and edited the *Daily American*, the first African-American daily newspaper in the United States. Three years later, he became the first African-American lawyer licensed to practice law in Florida.

In 1901, Johnson moved to New York City, where he and his brother, John Rosamond, wrote more than two hundred songs. One, called "You're All Right, Teddy," was used in Theodore Roosevelt's 1904 presidential campaign. After Roosevelt was elected, Johnson was appointed to diplomatic posts in Venezuela and later in Nicaragua. He also wrote a book called *The Autobiography of an Ex-Coloured Man*—so titled even though it was a novel, not an autobiography. In the book he condemned racial injustice.

After Woodrow Wilson was elected president, Johnson returned to the United States, where he finished writing a book of poetry called *Fifty Years and Other Poems*. He also joined the NAACP. In 1917, a riot broke out involving African-American soldiers stationed in Houston, Texas. After a hurried trial by court-martial, thirteen soldiers were secretly condemned to death and executed. When the news got out, Johnson led a bitter protest that forced President Wilson to change the death sentences to a less severe punishment in ten other cases. As a field secretary for the NAACP, Johnson increased the organization's membership, denounced the occupation of Haiti by U.S. Marines, and organized a "Silent March" against lynching. Continuing to write, he used his position as editor of the NAACP's *Crisis* magazine to promote the work of African-American writers and artists.

One of Johnson's songs, "Lift Every Voice and Sing," is often called the "Negro National Anthem." His own voice was one of those lifted to help African-Americans who could not speak for themselves.

Elizabeth "Bessie" Coleman

Pilot
1896–1926

Bessie Coleman was the first African-American woman aviator, but she had to leave the country to get her pilot's license.

Coleman was born in Atlanta, Texas, the twelfth of thirteen children. Her mother was African-American, and her father was three-quarters Choctaw Indian.

While Coleman was still a baby, her family moved to Waxahachie, Texas, where she grew up. Because Coleman was good in math, her mother gave her the chore of keeping the family's financial records. She also allowed Coleman to keep the money she earned washing clothes for her college education. It was enough to pay for one year at the Colored Agricultural and Normal University in Langston, Oklahoma.

In 1918, soldiers, including Coleman's brother Johnny, began returning home after fighting in World War I. They often talked about the exciting new airplanes they had seen. Coleman knew she had to learn to fly. But where? U.S. flying schools were segregated; they refused both African-Americans and women. However, with the help of two people—Robert

Sengstacke Abbott, founder of the *Chicago Defender,* and Jesse Binga, president of the Binga State Bank—Coleman was able to attend flying school in France. She received her pilot's license on June 15, 1921, from the Federation Aeronautique Internationale.

Coleman returned to the United States and began what was known as barnstorming—participating in stunt-flying exhibitions at state fairs, circuses, carnivals, and other events. Known as "Queen Bess," Coleman ruled the skies with her daring performances. But no matter how high she flew, Coleman never forgot the African-Americans on the ground. She insisted that her audiences be integrated, and once refused to perform until other pilots dropped notices across the city letting African-Americans know they were welcome to attend her performance. She also gave speeches at black churches and schools encouraging African-American children to fly.

Though Coleman dreamed of establishing her own aviation school, it was not to be. In 1926, she was killed when the controls on her plane jammed while she was practicing her performance for a Negro Welfare League benefit show in Jacksonville, Florida. Today, she is one of the few women featured in the Black Heritage postal stamp series. Every Memorial Day, African-American pilots fly over the Chicago Lincoln Cemetery, where Coleman rests, and drop a wreath on her grave.

Marcus Garvey

Black Nationalist
1887–1940

Action, self-reliance, the vision of self and the future have been the only means by which the oppressed have seen and realized the light of their own freedom.

—Marcus Garvey

Born in St. Ann's Bay, Jamaica, Marcus Garvey was the youngest of eleven children. Although he was a good student, financial problems forced him to leave school at fourteen and become a printer's apprentice. After helping organize a strike, Garvey was fired from his job. He worked briefly on a banana plantation in Costa Rica and for a newspaper in Panama, and then went to London, England.

In London, Garvey worked for a publisher and studied at night at the University of London. There he met a number of Africans who involved him in their independence movement. When he returned to Jamaica in 1914, Garvey organized the Universal Negro Improvement and Conservation Association and African Communities League (UNIA), with the intention of making Africa "the defender of Negroes the world over."

Intending to open a school in Jamaica, Garvey accepted an invitation to visit Booker T. Washington's school at Tuskegee, Alabama. When he arrived in the United States, however, he found that Washington had died. Throughout the following years, Garvey toured the United States, speaking about UNIA and the promise of a glorious black future in Africa. It was a message that attracted thousands of followers.

Garvey did more than talk. In 1918, he began publishing the *Negro World*, which soon became one of the most popular African-American newspapers in the United States. He established the Black Star Line steamship company, the Negro Factories Corporation, the Black Cross Nurses, the African Legion, and the Black Eagle Flying Corps. Within two years, he had raised more than $10 million.

In August 1920, Garvey staged a month-long convention in Harlem, New York, featuring bands, receptions, rallies, and parades. Thousands attended from twenty-five countries and all forty-eight states. Before it ended, the delegates voted to create an African government with Garvey at its head and to organize 400 million black people of the world into a free republic of Africa.

Unfortunately, before Garvey could realize any of his plans, his Black Star Line steamship company went bankrupt, and he was arrested for mail fraud in connection with the sale of Black Star stock. Convicted of the crime, fined $1,000, and ordered to serve a five-year jail sentence, Garvey entered Atlanta Penitentiary in 1925. Two years later, President Calvin Coolidge reduced his sentence and ordered him deported to Jamaica.

Garvey retired to London in 1935, where he died on June 10, 1940, following a stroke. His ambitious plans had failed, but he had captured the imagination of millions of black people as no other leader had before him.

Although his dream faded, Garvey's words remain sharp and clear: "Lose not courage, go forward . . . and you will compel the world to respect you."

Harlem Renaissance
Approximately 1919–1930

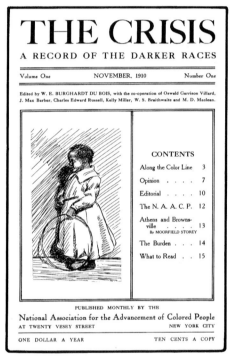

The Harlem Renaissance was the period from 1919 to 1930 during which there was an outpouring of African-American literature, art, music, and political and philosophical thought. During and after World War I, thousands of southern blacks moved north in search of jobs and opportunity. Many of these people ended up in Harlem in New York City. The atmosphere there was lively and exciting. Writers, artists, musicians, poets, actors, dancers, and political activists were encouraged to pursue their dreams—and they did.

This period was called a *renaissance,* a French word meaning "rebirth," because African-American creativity was once again able to shine after many years of repression. This was in part due to the support black artists received from African-American civil rights organizations. Both the NAACP and the National Urban League published magazines, such as The *Crisis,* that promoted the work of African-American writers, artists, and entertainers. Community leaders encouraged white publishers to support the work of black writers. They also arranged for black artists to get grant money so they could pursue their careers.

But in 1929, the stock market crashed, and thousands of people all over the country lost their savings. The Great Depression of the 1930s followed. Millions of people were unemployed, and financial support for African-American writers, artists, and others dried up. Although many continued to write or paint, hundreds of others were forced to postpone their dreams as they tried to find work to support themselves.

The Harlem Renaissance was a special time that encouraged the expression of African-American culture and thought. Population shifts brought together people from different backgrounds. Social change, along with financial and political support, created a dynamic atmosphere where all kinds of talent could flourish.

Louis Armstrong

Jazz Musician

1901–1971

Louis Armstrong's musical career started with a bang when he was arrested for firing a pistol on New Year's Eve in 1913. The judge sent thirteen-year-old Armstrong to the Colored Waif's Home for Boys, where he learned to play the cornet. When he was released, he began playing in local jazz bands. Since he didn't earn enough money as a musician, he was forced to take additional jobs hauling coal, washing dishes, and collecting junk.

Poverty was nothing new to Armstrong. He was born into a poor family in New Orleans in August 1901. His parents separated shortly afterward, leaving him to be raised by his grandmother until he was five or six years old.

Armstrong grew up in a section of the city famous for its bands and musicians. At age nine, he was singing on street corners for pennies. After he learned to play the cornet, a musician named Joe "King" Oliver took an interest in him and began to help him with his technique.

At eighteen, Armstrong quit his other jobs and began playing the cornet full time. He spent a year playing with an orchestra on a Mississippi riverboat. In 1922, Oliver, who had left New Orleans several years earlier, convinced Armstrong to join him in Chicago. Within a few months, Armstrong was more popular than Oliver. After a nationwide tour with Oliver's band, people started calling Armstrong one of the best musicians in the United States.

In 1924, Armstrong was invited to New York City to join the Fletcher Henderson Orchestra, which included some of the finest musicians in the country. While in New York, he switched from the cornet to the trumpet, the instrument for which he is best known.

When Armstrong returned to Chicago, he organized his own band, Louis Armstrong and the Hot Five. Later, the band expanded and became the Hot Seven. Many of their numbers became famous, such as "Gut Bucket Blues," "Heebie Jeebies," "Potato Head Blues," "Struttin with Some Barbeque," and "West End Blues."

Returning again to New York, Armstrong became a star in the musical *Hot Chocolates*. Later, he toured Europe, where he played for England's King George VI. He also toured Latin America and the Middle East. When he toured Africa in 1960, 100,000 people in Ghana came to hear him play. He was so popular that he became known as "America's Ambassador of Goodwill."

Known for his rich, warm tones, inventive melodies, and powerful solos, Armstrong also became famous for his gruff singing voice and for scatting—improvisational singing that uses meaningless syllables instead of words. Fondly nicknamed "Satchelmouth," or "Satchmo," Armstrong recorded numerous albums with such artists as Ella Fitzgerald and made more than fifty movies. When Armstrong died in 1971, music lovers everywhere mourned.

Zora Neale Hurston

Writer, Anthropologist
1901–1960

Zora Neale Hurston was flamboyant, controversial, and talented. The author of short stories, plays, essays, novels, and many newspaper and magazine articles, she was the most widely published African-American woman of her time and a leading figure during the Harlem Renaissance.

Hurston grew up in the small town called Eatonville, Florida. Her mother died when she was young, and she lived with various relatives until age fourteen, when she was forced to leave school and go to work. At sixteen, Hurston joined a traveling theater. Shortly afterward, she went to work for a white family in Baltimore, Maryland, and entered Morgan Academy, graduating in 1918. She then began taking courses at Howard University in Washington, D.C. In 1921, her short story "John Redding Goes to the Sea" was published in *The Stylus,* Howard's literary magazine.

Four years later, Hurston moved to New York, where she attracted the attention of Professor Alain Locke, who included her story "Spunk" in his famous anthology *The New Negro,* published in 1925. That same year, Hurston began studying anthropology at Barnard College. Her interest in black culture and folklore took her to Jamaica, Haiti, Central America, and the American South. Much of what Hurston learned appeared in her non-fiction books, including *Mules and Men* (1935) and *Tell My Horse* (1938). She also continued to write stories and novels. In 1937, Hurston published what would become her most famous novel, *Their Eyes Were Watching God.*

Hurston had grown up surrounded by an African-American community that was able to avoid much of the day-to-day discrimination and harassment that others were forced to endure. As an adult, she declared her color was a blessing that provided her with the opportunity to know and enjoy all that black culture had to offer. This attitude led to her her criticism of integration and her refusal to see African-Americans as victims. In fact, Hurston later criticized the *Brown v. Board of Education* Supreme Court school desegregation decision as implying that African-American children could not learn in an all-black environment.

In time, the power of Hurston's writing has overcome her controversial political views. Her love and respect for African-American culture and people has made her a favorite among many readers. Her autobiography, published in 1942, is titled *Dust Tracks on a Road.*

Langston Hughes

Writer

1902–1967

Langston Hughes's father left home shortly after Langston's birth in Joplin, Missouri. As a result, Hughes spent much of his childhood with his grandmother, Mary Langston. Mary's first husband was Lewis Sheridan Leary, an abolitionist who was killed while fighting at Harpers Ferry. All Mary had to remember him by was the shawl he was wearing when he died. Often, she would wrap herself in the blood-stained, bullet-riddled cloth and tell young Langston stories about the lives of Frederick Douglass, Harriet Tubman, and other freedom fighters.

Mother to Son ·—·

Well, son, I'll tell you:
Life for me ain't been no crystal stair.
It's had tacks in it,
And splinters,
And boards torn up,
And places with no carpet on the floor—
Bare.
But all the time
I'se been a-climbing on,
And reachin' landin's,

And turnin' corners,
And sometimes goin' in the dark
Where there ain't been no light.
So boy, don't you turn back.
Don't you set down on the steps
'Cause you finds it's kinder hard.
Don't you fall now—
For I'se still goin', honey,
I'se still climbin',
And life for me ain't been no crystal stair.

·—·

Sometimes at night, she would tenderly wrap the shawl around him as he slept. From these childhood memories came the strong African-American pride that later flowed through all of Hughes's writing.

At thirteen, Hughes started reading the poetry of Claude McKay, Carl Sandburg, and Walt Whitman. Following their example, he began to compose his own poetry. At nineteen, his poem "The Negro Speaks of Rivers" was published in the *Crisis,* one of the most influential African-American magazines in the country. In it, he affirms his link to his African heritage. Originally scribbled on the back of an old envelope, the poem was to become one of his most famous.

In 1921, Hughes enrolled at Columbia University in New York City. Although he did well at Columbia, he was more interested in Harlem, where African-American music, theater, art, and literature were flourishing during the Harlem Renaissance. Leaving college after only one year, he took several menial jobs and then signed on as a sailor on an old freighter.

Life on board ship suited Hughes, and he wrote poem after poem. After traveling to Africa and Europe, he jumped ship and lived for a while in Paris, where he spent hours listening to the black musicians who had moved there to work. Back in the United States, he continued to frequent the nightclubs where African-American musicians performed and to visit storefront churches. Hughes was caught up in the rhythms of the sermons, spirituals, and hymns: "Like the waves of the sea coming one after another . . . so is the undertow of black music with its rhythm that never betrays you, its strength like the beat of the human heart, its humor and its rooted power."

In 1924, Hughes moved to Washington, D.C., where he got a job as a busboy at the Wardman Park Hotel. When he found that poet Vachel Lindsay was staying at the Wardman, he arranged to show him some of his poems. Lindsay was so impressed that he read Hughes's poems to an audience that night. The response was overwhelming, and Hughes was invited to do his own reading.

Hughes's first book of poetry, *The Weary Blues,* was published in 1926. The same year, he enrolled at Lincoln University near Philadelphia, graduating in 1929. While in school, he still found time to write poetry. Some African-American critics felt his second book, published in 1927, glorified immorality and showed African-Americans in a bad light. Hughes defended himself, saying, "I have the right to portray any side of Negro life I wish to . . . every 'ugly' poem I write is a protest against the ugliness it pictures."

Hughes's first novel, *Not Without Laughter* (1930), was an immediate success. During this time, Hughes traveled widely and spent a year in Russia. After returning home, he wrote a number of short stories that were collected in *The Ways of White Folks* (1934).

Three years later, as a newspaper correspondent, Hughes covered the Spanish civil war. When he returned home, he established the Harlem Suitcase Theatre. Its opening production—his own one-act play, *Don't You Want to Be Free?*—was a huge success. He later founded two other theaters, one in Los Angeles and another in Chicago.

In 1934, Hughes began writing a regular news column in which he presented the shrewd, humorous views of an African-American man named Jesse B. Semple, or "Simple." The Simple Stories, later collected into five books, are now considered to be among his best work.

In all of his writing, Hughes celebrated ordinary African-American working people. He liked them, felt at ease with them, and respected them. His work is notable for both its quality and its quantity. Over the years, he wrote not only poetry, but also plays, novels, children's books, short stories, histories, biographies, radio and TV scripts, and his own autobiography. Known as the "Poet Laureate of Harlem," Hughes is primarily considered a poet. Often humorous, sometimes militant, occasionally subdued, his writing mirrored his observations, his beliefs and, most of all, his hopes.

Alain Leroy Locke

Philosopher, Educator, Writer
1885–1954

Since his parents were both school-teachers, it is not surprising that Alain Locke was an excellent student. He graduated *magna cum laude* (with highest honors) from Harvard University after just three years. In 1907, he became the first African-American to be awarded a Rhodes Scholarship to study in England. He also studied at the University of Berlin in Germany. This was particularly important because it came at a time when many whites were trying to prove that African-Americans were inferior intellectually, and segregation was therefore necessary.

Locke returned to the United States in 1911, and a year later he began teaching at Howard University in Washington, D.C. After receiving his Ph.D. from Harvard, he became chairman of Howard's philosophy department. In 1924, Locke traveled to Egypt. When he returned to Howard, he found an ongoing dispute about faculty salaries and other issues. Because of the complaints, Locke and several other professors were dismissed in June 1925. His firing resulted in many protests from alumni and others, and he was later reinstated.

That same year, Locke was asked to edit a special issue of a magazine called *Survey Graphic*. He took the opportunity to highlight the work of

African-American authors and intellectuals. It was a huge success, and Locke decided to expand his idea of showcasing African-American authors in a book called *The New Negro* (1925). The book made Locke a leader of the Harlem Renaissance. He continued to work closely with African-American artists and writers during this period.

After Locke returned to Howard in 1928, he encouraged the study of African and African-American studies and helped arrange a forty-year series of conferences on racial issues sponsored by the University's Division of the Social Sciences. He took a leading role in reforming Howard's liberal arts curriculum and promoting adult education. Locke is now considered one of the leading African-American scholars of the twentieth century.

Carter G. Woodson

Historian
1875–1950

The oldest of nine children, Carter G. Woodson's small income as a coal miner was important in helping his family get by. Largely self-educated, he went to high school part-time so he could work. Woodson graduated after a year and a half and entered Berea College in Kentucky. While still an undergraduate, he began teaching in West Virginia and became principal of Douglass High School in Fayette County. After receiving his degree from Berea in 1903, he left for the Philippines, where he worked as a teacher and learned to speak Spanish. He also traveled to Europe, Asia, and North Africa, and spent a semester at the University of Paris.

In 1908, Woodson received his degree from the University of Chicago. He then became the first African-American with slave parents to earn a Ph.D. from Harvard. He began teaching Spanish, French, English, and history at Dunbar High School in Washington, D.C. At that time the schools in Washington were segregated, and Dunbar was considered the best African-American school in the city.

In 1915, Woodson and three other men founded the Association for the Study of Negro Life and History (ASNLH). The purpose of the organization was to promote interest in African-American history and educate the public about blacks' achievements. A year later, he began publication of the *Journal of Negro History*. It was difficult to find sufficient financial support for the *Journal* and ASNLH, but Woodson refused to affiliate with any university or organization that might force him to accept white influence. He remained editor of the *Journal* until his death in 1950.

In 1922, Woodson started what would be his life's work: researching, writing, and promoting public interest in African-American history. He began by setting up a publishing company. Over the years he wrote hundreds of articles, books, and papers on African-American history and culture. In 1926, Woodson proclaimed Black History Week, which later became Black History Month. He encouraged people like Zora Neale Hurston, Mary McLeod Bethune, and W. E. B. Du Bois to write articles for his journal and provided a great deal of educational material to African-American teachers. For his efforts, he is known as the "Father of Black History."

Edward Kennedy "Duke" Ellington

Musician, Composer, Bandleader
1899–1974

*You go home expecting to go right to bed. . . .
On the way, you [pass] the piano. . . . You sit
down and try out a couple of chords. . . . When
you look up it's 7 A.M.*

—Duke Ellington

At one time his mother had to force him to practice the piano. By the time of his death at age seventy-five, Duke Ellington had become one of America's greatest composers. His musical legacy encompassed almost six thousand pieces, including more than two thousand jazz compositions, musicals, concert pieces, film scores, a ballet, and hymns.

Born Edward Kennedy Ellington in Washington, D.C., he was nicknamed "Duke" because of the flashy way he liked to dress—always "duked out." As a boy, he was more interested in baseball and art than in music. When he finished high school, the Pratt Institute in New York City offered him an art scholarship. By that time, however, music had become more important to him.

Ellington's interest in music began at the Poodle Dog Café, where he worked behind the soda fountain after school. The café had a small band, and Ellington was sometimes asked to sit in. At seventeen, he composed his first piece, "The Soda Fountain Rag." Not long afterward, he began playing professionally.

Sometimes Ellington's creativity led to trouble. Once, Russell Wooding hired him to play one of five pianos in his orchestra. Four of the pianists played as they were supposed to—in unison. Ellington, however, decided the piece would sound better if he improvised. The audience loved it, but Wooding did not. He told Ellington to improvise elsewhere and fired him.

Ellington was not about to change his style. Instead, he formed his own band, the Washingtonians. In 1922, they tried their luck in New York City. Ellington met several musicians there, including Willie "the Lion" Smith and Fats Waller, both of whom influenced his technique. The trip was unsuccessful, however, and the band returned home. In 1923, they returned to New York and opened at the Hollywood Club at Forty-ninth Street and Broadway.

A 1927 show at Harlem's famous Cotton Club marked a major turning point in Ellington's career. The Cotton Club was the location of a regular radio broadcast. Before long, Ellington's theme song, "East St. Louis Toodle-Oo," was heard nationwide. In the five years he played at the Cotton Club, Ellington produced some of his most memorable music, including "Mood Indigo," "The Mooche," and "Rocking in Rhythm."

After leaving the Cotton Club, the Ellington band toured Europe and appeared in several movies. In spite of the pressures of the Great Depression and World War II, Ellington continued to compose. Among the famous pieces he wrote at this time were "Solitude," "Sophisticated Lady," "Black, Brown, and Beige," and "Take the A Train."

As his fame spread, Ellington was asked to perform at major concert halls, such as the New York Metropolitan Opera House. Success never changed him, however. Ellington's first loyalty was always to his band and his music. During the 1950s, when support for bands dropped off and many groups split up, Ellington insisted on keeping his band together: "I like to keep a band so I can write and hear the music the next day. A musical profit is more important than a financial loss."

Charles Hamilton Houston

Law Professor
1895–1950

Do not lose heart if victory does not come at once.
Persevere to the end.

—Charles Hamilton Houston

The Civil Rights Movement of the 1950s and 1960s drew on a legal framework shaped in part by Charles Hamilton Houston. Houston was born in Washington, D.C. A brilliant student, he graduated Phi Beta Kappa (an honor society) from Amherst College in Massachusetts. He taught English for several years, then entered the Army. When his tour of duty was over, Houston entered Harvard Law School, where he became the first African-American elected to *Law Review,* a legal journal open only to the best students in the class. He said he wanted to "study law and use my time fighting for men who could not strike back."

After his graduation, Houston returned to Washington, where he opened a private law practice. He also began teaching at Howard University Law School. At age thirty-four, he became dean of the school. In an effort to upgrade the school's standards, he closed the night school, raised admission requirements, and brought in new faculty. He then set out to create a law school that would train African-American lawyers dedicated to winning equal rights. One of his students was Thurgood Marshall, who would one day win the case outlawing segregation in public schools and later become a Supreme Court justice.

In 1935, Houston took a leave of absence from Howard to work for the NAACP. At both the NAACP and at Howard, he played a major role in deciding what legal strategy should be used in many important civil rights cases. His work helped convince judges to rule for the NAACP in cases that protested the unlawful exclusion of African-Americans from juries, unfair housing practices, union discrimination, and school segregation. More important, Houston was responsible for inspiring dozens of lawyers to spend their careers working for civil rights.

Jesse Owens
Olympic Track and Field Athlete
1913–1980

Three years before World War II began, a twenty-two-year-old man named Jesse Owens handed Adolf Hitler a crushing defeat. The scene was the 1936 Olympics in Berlin, Germany. Owens, competing for the United States, had won four gold medals in the 100- and 200-meter events, long jump, and 400-meter relay. Hitler had long held that the Nazis were racially superior to blacks, Jews, and everyone else in the world. Owens, in what was later called the most important sports event of the century, proved him wrong.

Owens was born James Cleveland Owens on September 12, 1913, in Danville, Alabama. He was the seventh of eleven children. Desperately poor, he began picking cotton at the age of seven. Back then, running was the farthest thing from his mind. After the family moved to Cleveland, Ohio, however, he began running track in high school. When he was recruited by Ohio State University, Owens continued to run while he worked at several jobs to pay his tuition fees. His first two initials, "J.C.," got shortened to his nickname "Jesse."

On May 25, 1935, Owens competed in the Big Ten College Track-and-Field Championships at Ann Arbor, Michigan. Within 45 minutes, he broke three world records and tied a fourth. People who watched him said, "It was

Jesse Owens prepares for a race.

one of those rare moments in sports when you can't believe what you are seeing." A reporter for the *Los Angeles Times* wrote, "No one before or since has ever had a day like that and no one probably ever will." What made Owens's success even more amazing was that he competed while suffering from a painful back injury.

Owens's outstanding performance a year later at the Olympics made him one of the most famous athletes in history. When he returned from Germany, thousands of Americans greeted him with a ticker-tape parade. Although he enjoyed his celebrity status, Owens needed more than parades and cheers. His wife, Ruth, whom he had married while still a teenager, was pregnant with their second child, and Owens needed a job.

Unable to finish college because of a lack of money, Owens took a job as a playground instructor earning $30 a week. When he was offered money to compete against a racehorse in a 100-yard dash, he accepted it. The money he earned from the race enabled him to return to college to get his degree.

Owens was offered other business ventures. He became part owner of a chain of cleaning stores. For a while, the business was profitable, but when his partners disappeared in 1938, he was left with debts of $55,000. To pay them off, he took a job with the Ford Motor Company. "I buckled down," he said, "and proved to myself that I had the talent to think as well as to run."

In 1949, the Owens family moved to Chicago, where Jesse went into the public relations business. Traveling extensively, he spoke to thousands of people about how athletic competition could improve racial problems and bring people together. In 1976, President Gerald Ford awarded Owens the Medal of Freedom.

Although he had set seven world records during his career, nothing was as meaningful to Owens as his Olympic victory. In a 1936 *Time* article, he recalls,

> Ralph Metcalfe of Marquette University still was ahead of me at 70 meters, and 120,000 people were roaring. Between 70 and 90 meters, Ralph and I were streaking neck and neck. Then I was in front at the finish. My eyes blurred as I heard the "Star Spangled Banner" played, first faintly and then loudly, and then I saw the American flag slowly raised for my victory.

Billie Holiday
1915–1959

Ella Fitzgerald
1918–1996

Jazz Singers

Billie Holiday

Billie Holiday grew up poor in Baltimore, Maryland. Her wonderful talent surfaced early, however, and she began singing for money while still in her early teens. Holiday was strongly influenced by singer Bessie Smith and musician Louis Armstrong. In 1933, she recorded her first album. Two years later she made another record with Teddy Wilson and several other musicians, including saxophonist Lester Young, who gave her the nickname "Lady Day." Holiday's career began to take off.

In 1937, Holiday began performing with the Count Basie band, then went on to work with white bandleader Artie Shaw. In accepting the job with Shaw, Holiday became one of the first African-American performers to work with an all-white group. This sometimes caused racial conflict with audiences, but Holiday was not afraid of controversy. One of her best-known songs was "Strange Fruit," written by Lewis Allan. "Strange Fruit" is about lynching. The title is a symbolic way of referring to the bodies of murder victims hanging from trees.

Problems with drug addiction forced Holiday to enter a rehabilitation clinic in 1947. Just three weeks after she was released, she was arrested for drug possession and sentenced to a year in jail. Following her release, her license to perform in clubs in New York was revoked, which seriously damaged her career. In 1952, Holiday signed with Norman Granz's Verve Records and recorded close to a hundred songs for the label. She died in 1959, partly as a result of her drug habit.

Ella Fitzgerald

Like Holiday, Ella Fitzgerald is considered one of the great jazz singers of the twentieth century. Born in Newport News, Virginia, she was orphaned at an early age and grew up in New York City. As a young girl in 1934, she won an amateur contest at Harlem's Apollo Theatre, and her prize was a chance to work with drummer and band director William "Chick" Webb. Webb was so impressed with Fitzgerald's talent that he asked her to join his group. She did, and while working with him recorded two of her most famous songs, "A-tisket, A-tasket" and "Undecided."

When Webb died in 1939, Fitzgerald took over his band and led the group for the next three years. She then began working with Norman Granz and toured the United States, Europe, South America, and the Far East. Like Holiday, Fitzgerald signed with Norman Granz's Verve Records and produced a series of hits.

Famous for her musical flexibility, melodic improvisation, and scat singing, Fitzgerald is known as the "First Lady of Jazz."

Richard Wright

Writer
1908–1960

The impulse to dream was slowly beaten out of me by experience. Now it surged up again and I hungered for books, new ways of looking and seeing.

—Richard Wright

When Richard Wright was four years old, he accidentally set the house on fire. As his punishment, he was beaten so badly that he lost consciousness and almost died. When he grew older, he suffered not from beatings but from poverty and hunger.

Hoping for a better life, the Wrights moved from Mississippi to Memphis, Tennessee, when Richard was very young. Shortly after they arrived there, Wright's father deserted the family. After he left, there was never enough to eat. At one point, things were so bad that Wright's mother placed him and his younger brother in an orphanage. Unhappy, he ran away but soon was caught. Shortly after this incident, his mother took her two boys to live with relatives in Arkansas.

The murder of Richard's uncle, and his mother's subsequent stroke, forced the Wrights to move again. This time they moved to Jackson, Mississippi, to live with Richard's grandmother. The next few years were unhappy ones. Wright could not get along with his grandmother, and the family had very little to eat.

One encouraging thing about living in Jackson was that Wright was able to attend school regularly. Although his mother taught him to read, he had little formal schooling before the age of twelve. His love of reading and vivid imagination inspired him to become a writer. In the segregated society in which he lived, however, such an ambitious goal seemed impossible for a poor African-American child.

Discrimination and racial hostility tore at Wright's self-respect. He dreamed of saving enough money to leave Jackson, but the menial jobs he managed to get did little more than provide him with food money. One day, in desperation, he stole a gun and some fruit preserves. With the money he made from selling them, he bought a ticket to Memphis.

In Memphis, Wright found work in an optical shop. Borrowing a library card from a friendly white man, he began reading whenever he could. Although he had gone no farther than the ninth grade, he soon became familiar with the writings of many of America's finest authors.

About 1927, Wright moved to Chicago, hoping to find greater freedom and opportunity. He worked as a dishwasher, porter, postal clerk, and insurance salesman. But when the depression crippled the U.S. economy in the 1930s, Wright, like thousands of others, found himself unemployed. Frustrated and miserable, he joined the Communist Party, which promised racial justice. In 1944, he quit the party, believing that the Communists were using African-Americans more than they were helping them.

Wright's dream of becoming a writer began to come true after he moved to New York City in 1937. Within a year, a collection of his stories, *Uncle Tom's Children*, was published. These stories reflect the prejudice and discrimination Wright experienced while growing up in the South. Two years later, with the support of a Guggenheim Fellowship, his most famous novel,

Native Son, was published. It sold 200,000 copies in fewer than three weeks and established Wright as one of the country's leading authors. Unlike his earlier work, which portrays the rural South, *Native Son* explores racism and oppression in the North as it affects a young African-American man named Bigger Thomas.

Following the success of *Native Son,* Wright completed a folk history called *Twelve Million Black Voices.* In 1945, he finished *Black Boy,* the story of his childhood and youth. Even more popular than *Native Son,* this book reveals the terrible poverty and racism that stunted the lives of most southern African-American children at that time.

Following his move to Paris in 1946, Wright became the leader of a group of writers, artists, and other intellectuals. He wrote *The Outsiders* in 1953 and *The Long Dream* in 1958. In 1961, *Eight Men* was published, a book that includes his famous story "The Man Who Lived Underground." His second autobiography, *American Hunger,* was published in 1977 after his death.

Wright is considered one of the finest authors this country has ever produced. His insights into American society shocked the public and exposed the terrible effects of racial prejudice. Starved, beaten, and rejected as a child, and forced to face unrelenting racial prejudice and discrimination as an adult, Wright made his way north and then overseas. He persevered, he said,

> full of a hazy notion that life could be lived with dignity, that the personalities of others should not be violated, that men should be able to confront other men without fear or shame, and that if men were lucky in their living on earth they might win some redeeming meaning for their having struggled and suffered here beneath the stars.

Julian Francis Abele
1881–1950

Paul Revere Williams
1894–1980

Architects

Julian Francis Abele

The lines are all Mr. Trumbauer's, but the shadows are all mine.

—Julian Abele as quoted by Michael Adams
in "A Legacy of Shadows"

African-Americans helped build this country, and in the case of Julian Abele and Paul Williams, they helped design it as well. In 1902, Abele became the first African-American to graduate from the University of Pennsylvania's School of Fine Arts and Architecture. He then traveled to Europe, where he spent four years studying at L'Ecole des Beaux-Arts in Paris. His work attracted the attention of Horace Trumbauer, a leading architect in Philadelphia. When Abele returned to the United States, he joined Trumbauer's architecture firm, and the two men worked closely together for thirty-one years.

Abele often vacationed in Europe, where he spent many hours sketching

Paul Revere Williams

Gothic cathedrals and other buildings that influenced his own designs. He became Trumbauer's chief designer and was responsible for much of the firm's most important work. This includes the design for the Institute of Fine Arts at New York University, Harvard's Widener Library, much of Duke University, and the Philadelphia Museum of Art.

Paul Revere Williams was an orphan. His high school teacher in Los Angeles tried to discourage him when he said he wanted to be an architect, but Williams refused to give up. He worked his way through the University of Southern California, then spent two years studying at the Beaux-Arts Institute in New York. He then returned to Los Angeles and, in 1923, opened his own architecture firm.

In 1926, Williams became the first African-American member of the American Institute of Architects. His work won many awards and prizes, and President Calvin Coolidge appointed him to the National Monument Commission. He designed the Palm Springs Tennis Club and the homes of many movie stars, including Frank Sinatra.

The work of both Abele and Williams is still admired for its beauty and elegance.

Paul Robeson

Actor, Singer, Political Activist
1898–1976

An artist must elect to fight for freedom or for slavery. I have made my choice.

—Paul Robeson

The son of an escaped slave, Paul Robeson was born in Princeton, New Jersey, in 1898. When he was seventeen, he won a scholarship to Rutgers University. There he won twelve letters in baseball, basketball, and track and was twice named first Black All-American in football. While still a junior, Robeson was elected to Phi Beta Kappa, the national college honor society for outstanding students. He graduated in 1919 and was class valedictorian.

After graduation, Robeson played professional football on weekends to support himself while he attended Columbia University Law School. He graduated in 1923, receiving his law degree in only two years. By this time he had become interested in acting.

When famous playwright Eugene O'Neill saw Robeson act, he asked him to play the lead in his play *All God's Chillun Got Wings*. Robeson's performance was well received. In 1924, he joined the cast of O'Neill's masterpiece, *The Emperor Jones*, again receiving critical acclaim.

Robeson was also becoming known as a singer. Although he had little training, his voice was rich and powerful. After hearing him sing, Jerome

Kern gave him the part of "Joe" in the musical *Showboat*. Robeson's rendition of the song "Ol' Man River" became the hit of the show. In later years, he was often asked to perform it at concerts and other occasions.

Robeson was equally popular in Europe, where audiences jammed concert halls to hear him perform. In 1930, he went to England to star in Shakespeare's *Othello*. It became his most spectacular triumph. "Dignified, magnificent and black—Paul Robeson . . . made stage history," said one critic. When he toured the United States in the role, another said, "There has never been and never will be a finer rendition of this particular tragedy. It is unbelievably magnificent."

In the late 1930s, Robeson became concerned with politics. He was active in the peace movement, bettering labor conditions, and obtaining racial justice. His strong beliefs led him to picket the White House, protest lynching, refuse to sing before segregated audiences, and support communism.

As a result of his association with communism, Robeson was called before congressional investigative committees and blacklisted. Theater managers and stage and movie producers refused to hire him. In 1950, the State Department revoked his passport, making it impossible for him to work overseas. His income, which in 1947 had been $104,000, dropped to $2,000 annually.

In 1958, however, a Supreme Court ruling in a related case forced the State Department to return Robeson's passport. He tried to resume his acting and singing career, but illness forced him to quit. He lived quietly in Harlem and later in Philadelphia until his death in 1976.

Robeson once said, "As I went out into life, one thing loomed above all else: I was my father's son, a Negro in America. That was the challenge." This was a challenge Robeson was quick to meet.

Joe Louis

Heavyweight Boxing Champion
1914–1981

When he won, we all won. That's how African-Americans felt about Joe Louis—and luckily, he won most of the time. Called the "Brown Bomber," Louis became heavyweight champion at age 23 and defended his title 25 times—more than any other boxer in history. In all, 68 men went down before Louis's left jab and right hook.

Born in a tiny shack in Chamber County, Alabama, Joseph Louis Barrow was the fifth child of Lillie and Monroe Barrow. At age four, he was working with his mother in the cotton fields to help bring in money. Rarely able to attend school, he didn't begin to read and write until he was nine years old.

Louis began boxing when he was a teenager. In his first amateur bout, he was knocked down 7 times in 2 rounds—not a very good beginning. In his second bout, he won by a knockout. During his two years as an amateur light heavyweight, he won 48 of 54 fights by knockouts. About this time he dropped his last name, Barrow, and was known only as Joe Louis.

In 1934, Louis turned professional. His managers, John Roxborough and Julian Black, saw in him a future heavyweight champion of the world. They knew, however, that the battle to make him a champion would have to be fought outside the ring as well as inside it. White titleholders were sometimes reluctant to accept a challenge from a black contender, and riots often broke out when white boxers were defeated by African-Americans. Still, no one could ignore Louis.

In 1935, Louis went up against Primo Carnera, the "Man Mountain," who stood 6 feet, 6 inches (2 m) tall and weighed 250 pounds (113 kg). To prevent any trouble during the match, 1,300 policemen surrounded Yankee Stadium in New York where the bout was held. Three hundred undercover officers mingled with the crowd. Carnera went down in the sixth round, and the referee stopped the fight. Thousands of African-Americans jammed the streets of Harlem to celebrate the win.

In 1936, Louis was beaten by German boxer Max Schmeling. Adolf Hitler gloated, saying Louis's defeat proved Germans were superior to African-Americans. For Louis, it was a crushing defeat.

But he kept on fighting. In 1937, Louis won the heavyweight title when he defeated James Braddock. The win felt good, but he was still bothered by his loss to Schmeling. On June 22, 1938, he met Schmeling in the ring again. This time he won by a knockout in the first two minutes of the fight.

During World War II, Louis's fighting career was put on hold while he spent four years in the army. A few years later, on March 1, 1949, he officially retired from boxing. He had successfully defended his title for 11 years and 8 months—longer than any other man. In 71 professional bouts, he had been defeated only 3 times.

Loyal to his family and generous to his friends, Louis was idolized by people across the country. For millions of African-Americans who had little voice in society and could not make themselves heard, Louis's fists spoke for them.

Marian Anderson

Opera Singer
1897–1993

Everyone has a gift for something, even if the gift is that of being a good friend. Young people should try and set a goal for themselves, and see that everything they do has some relation to the ultimate attainment of that goal.

—Marian Anderson

In 1939, Marian Anderson, one of the most famous opera singers in the world, was barred from singing in Constitution Hall in Washington, D.C., because she was black. Constitution Hall was owned by the Daughters of the American Revolution (DAR). The organization, citing racial reasons, refused to let Anderson perform there.

The incident made headlines across the country. First Lady Eleanor Roosevelt resigned from the DAR in protest. On Easter Sunday, 1939, Anderson performed, instead, at the Lincoln Memorial in Washington, D.C. Seventy-five thousand people, including many diplomats and politicians, gathered to hear her. In response to the prejudice of the DAR, Anderson sang "The Star Spangled Banner," "America," "Ave Maria," and "My Soul Is Anchored in the Lord."

A quiet, dignified woman, Anderson had always loved music. As a little girl, she often scrubbed her neighbors' steps to earn money to buy a violin.

Marian Anderson performs on the steps of the Lincoln Memorial in 1939.

She began her music career singing in a choir at the Union Baptist Church in South Philadelphia, where she was born. Her wonderful contralto voice so impressed all who heard her that the congregation arranged for her to study with Giuseppe Boghetti, a world-famous voice teacher. Soon Anderson was singing professionally.

When Anderson was twenty, she was given a chance to sing at Town Hall in New York City. She was ill prepared, however, and the concert went badly. Anderson became so discouraged by this event that she came close to giving up singing. In 1925, however, she competed against other singers and won the Lewisohn Stadium Concert Award. Her success led to a concert tour and an appearance as a soloist with the New York Philharmonic Orchestra.

In the following years, Anderson toured Europe, South America, Asia, and the United States. She sang to standing-room-only crowds in countries throughout the world. In 1955, she became the first African-American to sing at the New York Metropolitan Opera House. Two years later, at the request of the U.S. State Department, she toured twelve Asian nations. Upon her return in 1958, President Dwight D. Eisenhower made her a member of the United States delegation to the United Nations in New York City.

By the time she retired in 1965, Anderson had received awards from the king of Sweden, the emperor of Japan, and the president of the United States. She had sung at the inaugurations of Presidents Dwight D. Eisenhower and John F. Kennedy. The reaction of the music world to her talent can be summed up by the great orchestra conductor Arturo Toscanini. Anderson's, he said, is the kind of voice that is "heard once in a hundred years."

Leroy Robert "Satchel" Paige

Baseball Pitcher
1906–1982

Don't look back. Something might be gaining on you.

—Satchel Paige

Born in Mobile, Alabama, Leroy Robert Paige developed his pitching arm by throwing rocks at chickens to kill them for the family dinner table. He got his nickname, "Satchel," as a young boy when he worked at the train station carrying suitcases, or satchels, for passengers.

Paige learned to play baseball when he was sentenced to five years at the Mount Meigs Industrial School for Negro Children for shoplifting. After he was released at age seventeen, he joined a semiprofessional team called the Mobile Tigers. They paid him a dollar a game—and if the team had no money, he got a keg of lemonade instead.

Paige's fastball and showmanship quickly made him a favorite with the fans. In 1926, he joined the Chattanooga Black Lookouts for $50 a month. In those days, African-American ballplayers played in a segregated Negro Baseball League, but Paige was such a great pitcher that the managers of white teams were envious. Stran Niglin, who ran the white Chattanooga Lookouts, once offered Paige $500 if he would paint himself white and pitch for him. Insulted, Paige turned him down. He said the fans would not have been fooled anyway—they knew no one else could pitch like he could.

In 1928, Paige joined the Birmingham Black Barons at $275 a month. He began his first game by telling his teammates he would strike out the first six batters in a row. After he struck out the first five, one of the men on the other team waved a white towel at Paige. The sixth batter was called out after a pop-up fly. When Paige's teammates pointed out that he had not lived up to his promise, Paige said, "I didn't need to. They'd already surrendered."

Paige liked to name his pitches. Besides his fastball, there was his "bee ball" ("because it be where I want it to be"), "trouble ball," "four-day rider," "bat dodger," "midnight creeper," and "hesitation pitch" (which was banned when no one could hit it). In addition to playing in the United States, he played in Puerto Rico, Venezuela, and the Dominican Republic.

Paige was bitter about the racial prejudice that kept him out of the major leagues until the end of his career. In spite of the injustice he suffered, Paige remained patriotic. When World War II broke out, he registered for the draft and even moved his birth date up to 1908 to improve the likelihood of his being called to serve. He also demanded that the team owners donate $10,000 from the gate receipts of the 1944 East-West All-Star game to wounded soldiers. When they would not, he refused to play.

In 1948, at the age of 42, Paige was signed by the Cleveland Indians, and his 6–1 winning record helped the Indians get to the World Series for the first time in 28 years. He retired in 1953 as the oldest man ever to play in the major leagues. Paige was elected to the Baseball Hall of Fame in Cooperstown in 1971. Many regard him as the best pitcher of all time.

Asa Philip Randolph

Union Organizer, Civil Rights Leader
1889–1979

The Negro should organize himself because with organization he will be better able to break down the barriers and prejudices of white workers against him than he will without.

—A. Philip Randolph

"Last hired, first fired." For millions of African-American workers, this was more than just an expression; it was a way of life that included low pay and poor working conditions. Not until A. Philip Randolph organized the Brotherhood of Sleeping Car Porters in 1925 did things begin to change.

Born in Crescent City, Florida, Randolph spent his early teens working first in his father's small tailor and cleaning shop, then as a newsboy, grocery clerk, railroad worker, and driver. After completing high school at Cookman Institute, he enrolled at the City College of New York. There, as he worked at several poorly paid jobs, he became concerned with the problems of African-American workers. He decided the answer to many of these problems lay in unionization. It was an answer many employers did not like. They did not want organizations to protect workers' rights. As a result, Randolph was often labeled a troublemaker and fired from his job.

During World War I, Randolph tried (but failed) to organize the shipyard workers. Later, he was successful in organizing the Pullman Company's railroad porters and maids. The formation of the Brotherhood of Sleeping Car Porters in 1925 was only the first step, however. The Pullman Company hired detectives to spy on workers and fired more than five hundred people who were active in the union. After a long and bitter fight, Pullman finally agreed to recognize the union in 1937 and negotiated a new employee contract.

When the United States entered World War II in 1941, thousands of African-Americans volunteered for the service. Placed in segregated units, black soldiers faced many of the same discriminatory practices common during World War I. In the private sector, African-Americans were refused jobs in defense industries because of their color. Determined to eliminate racial discrimination, Randolph threatened to lead a protest march on Washington, D.C., in July 1941. President Franklin Roosevelt called a conference of African-American leaders. As a result of this meeting, he issued Executive Order 8802, banning job discrimination in defense industries, and set up the Fair Employment Practices Committee.

Not until 1948 was the issue of discrimination in the armed services addressed. Then, President Harry Truman issued Executive Order 9981, stating, "There shall be equality of treatment and opportunity for all persons in the armed forces."

Throughout the 1950s, Randolph pressed for action against racial discrimination in labor organizations. In 1960, he established the Negro American Labor Council. Three years later, he organized and directed the famous 1963 March on Washington. It marked the highlight of his career, as over 250,000 marchers took to the streets to demand civil rights legislation.

The demands that Randolph set forth for African-American workers were simple: equal opportunity, equal pay, and equal treatment. No one in the labor movement did more than he to see those demands were met.

Charles Richard Drew

Physician, Scientist
1904–1950

Thousands of American soldiers lost their lives in World War II. But thousands more stayed alive—though gravely wounded—because of the medical research and dedication of Charles Richard Drew.

Born and raised in Washington, D.C., Drew attended Amherst College, where he was an All-American football player. Following graduation, he took a job at Morgan College as a biology teacher and athletics director.

Although Drew brought Morgan's basketball and football teams up to championship level, a medical career was what he really wanted. He applied to McGill University Medical School in Montreal, Canada, and was accepted. While there, he became interested in the study of blood and how to preserve it.

All people have one of four blood types: A, B, AB, or O. Should an injured person need a blood transfusion, it is important that the blood he receives be of his own type and that it match, or be compatible with, his own blood. In the 1930s, many patients died because not enough blood of the right type and match could be found quickly enough. The problem was further complicated by the fact that blood spoils rapidly, making it very difficult to store.

Drew became fascinated with the problem of preserving blood. Shortly after graduating from McGill, he moved to New York to do graduate study at Columbia Medical School and to work as a surgical resident at Presbyterian Hospital. While there, he performed numerous experiments on the physical, chemical, and biological changes that make blood unusable for transfusions. He learned that while whole blood could not be stored longer than one week, blood plasma (the liquid portion of the blood, without blood cells) kept much longer.

Meanwhile, the war raged in Europe. Nazi bombers were attacking England daily, and the number of casualties was growing steadily. In August 1940, the Blood for Britain project was set up to make more blood available. The program ran into serious trouble almost immediately. Different hospitals were using different standards for collecting and processing blood. As a result, much of the plasma reaching England was contaminated and had to be thrown out.

It was then that Drew received a cablegram from Dr. John Beattie, head of shock treatment and transfusions for the Royal Air Force in England. His emergency message asked Drew to ship 10,000 pints of plasma to him within one month. It seemed like an impossible task, but Drew did it. Soon afterward, he became the medical supervisor of the Blood for Britain program and standardized procedures for collecting, processing, storing, and shipping plasma.

Due to the success of his program, Drew was appointed Red Cross director of a nationwide project to collect blood for the U.S. military. The project was going well until the Red Cross decided it did not want any "colored" blood. Such a racist policy made no sense from any scientific or medical point of view. In an angry September 26, 1942, editorial, the *Chicago Defender* said:

No Negro blood accepted but—

When the terrible blitz raids of London . . . killed and wounded thousands . . . it was an American Negro surgeon [who organized] and [sent] U.S. blood plasma overseas.

No Negro blood accepted but—

When the Japanese bombed Pearl Harbor and maimed hundreds of American soldiers and sailors, it was blood collected by a Negro surgeon that saved their lives.

Because of this kind of protest, the military agreed to accept "colored" blood but insisted that it be kept separate from blood donated by whites. To Drew this directive was unacceptable, and he resigned from the blood program.

On April 1, 1950, Drew was killed in an automobile accident while on his way to a medical conference. Only a year earlier, he had been appointed surgical consultant for the U.S. Army European Theater of Operations. The Army, which had not wanted to accept his blood, had at least recognized the value of his advice.

Jackie Robinson
Baseball Player
1919–1972

There are many of us who attain what we want and forget those who help us along the line. . . . We've got to remember that there are so many others to pull along the way. The further they go, the further we all go.

—Jackie Robinson

In 1962, in his very first year of eligibility, Jackie Robinson was elected to the Baseball Hall of Fame. Although he had tremendous athletic ability, Robinson almost didn't make it to the major leagues.

At the time Robinson became active in baseball, the major leagues were open to white ballplayers only. African-Americans competed in a separate Negro League. In spite of continuing pressure from the African-American press and various civil rights organizations, little headway had been made in changing the situation.

Born in Cairo, Georgia, in 1919, Jack Roosevelt Robinson learned at an early age that life would be hard. When he was only a year old, his father deserted the family. His mother then packed up her five children and moved to Pasadena, California, where she found work as a maid. After graduating from high school, Robinson attended Pasadena Junior College and, later, UCLA. He became the first student to win letters in four different sports—

baseball, basketball, football, and track. During his third year at UCLA, however, he was forced to quit school and work to help support his family.

Soon after the Japanese bombed Pearl Harbor in World War II, Robinson was drafted into the Army. Stationed at Fort Riley, Kansas, he was denied entrance to the Officer's Candidate School (OCS) because he was black. Robinson protested vehemently, both to the Army and to world heavyweight champion Joe Louis, who was also stationed at Fort Riley. Louis used his influence with the War Department to convince the military command to change its policies.

After the war, Robinson signed a contract to play baseball for an African-American team called the Kansas City Monarchs. Meanwhile, Branch Rickey, president and general manager of the Brooklyn Dodgers, decided to integrate major league baseball. Moving secretly so as not to arouse opposition, he sent scouts to check out the Negro League teams and report back on outstanding players. Jackie Robinson's name kept coming up on the scouting reports.

On August 28, 1945, Branch Rickey and Robinson met. Rickey wanted to sign Robinson to the Dodgers, but first he had to know if Robinson could take the heat. A fight or ugly incident of any kind, even if Robinson were not at fault, could wreck their plans and set back their efforts to integrate the league. Could Robinson ignore the insults, threats, and deliberately thrown bean balls? The answer was yes!

In the spring of 1946, Robinson began playing with the Montreal Royals, the Dodgers's top farm club, and then joined the Dodgers the following year. These were rough years. Not only opposing players but also some of his teammates joined forces to make Robinson's life miserable. Several got up a petition protesting his presence. The president of the Philadelphia Phillies said his team would not play the Dodgers as long as Robinson remained on the roster. The St. Louis Cardinals threatened a protest strike. As reported in the May 9, 1947 *Herald Tribune,* Ford Frick, president of the National League, responded as follows:

> If you do this, you will be suspended from the league. . . . I do not care if half the league strikes. Those who do it will encounter quick retribution. They will be suspended, and I don't care if it wrecks the National League for five years. This is the United States of America, and one citizen has as much right to play as another. The National League will go down the line with Robinson whatever the consequence.

The Dodgers, with Robinson's help, won the National League pennant that year. On September 30, 1947, Robinson became the first African-American to compete in the World Series (the Yankees won). He was also named Rookie of the Year. In 1949, he led the league with a .342 average and won the Most Valuable Player Award.

In 1957, Robinson was traded to the Giants but retired a month later. His success with the Dodgers had opened the way for other African-American ballplayers to enter the major leagues.

Gordon Parks

Photographer, Movie Director, Writer
1912—

I didn't know what lay ahead of me, but I believed in myself.

—Gordon Parks, *A Choice of Weapons*

Gordon Parks was born in Fort Scott, Kansas. He was the youngest of fifteen children. His mother died when he fifteen years old, and he supported himself by working as a dish washer, piano player, farm hand, and waiter.

Life was hard. In 1929, the stock market crashed, bringing on the Great Depression. Jobs were hard to find, so Parks joined the Civilian Conservation Corps, a government program set up to provide work and job training for unemployed young people.

In 1938, Parks bought a used camera for $7.50, moved to Chicago, and began his career as a photographer. After working for the Farm Security Administration, taking pictures of poor people to provide a documentary history for a government agency, he received a World War II assignment to photograph members of the 332nd Fighter Group, an all-black unit of fighter pilots. In 1949, he joined the staff of *Life* magazine. Parks photographed everything from gang members in Harlem to fashion models in

Paris to poverty-stricken slum dwellers in Brazil. He covered the developing Civil Rights Movement, as well as the Black Power Movement.

Parks's first book, *The Learning Tree* (1963), is still listed on many school reading lists. *The Learning Tree* was made into a movie, which Parks directed, making him the first African-American director of a major feature film. Parks also directed *Flavio, Shaft, Shaft's Big Score, Diary of a Harlem Family,* and *The Super Cops.* He continued to write books and take pictures. For years, many Americans had considered the thoughts and feelings of African-Americans unimportant. Gordon Parks's photographs helped change that.

Percy Lavon Julian

Chemist
1899–1975

Although his discoveries saved thousands of people from blindness, many scientists were never able to see past Percy Lavon Julian's race.

Born in Montgomery, Alabama, in 1899, Julian struggled to obtain an education. Although he was accepted at DePauw University in Indiana, his high school education had been so inadequate that he was forced to take remedial courses along with his regular college courses. Nevertheless, he graduated with honors and was valedictorian of his class.

Julian wanted to continue his education, but racial prejudice kept him from being accepted at leading graduate schools. So he took a job at Fisk University teaching chemistry. Two years later, when he was accepted at Harvard University, he continued his studies in chemistry. After graduation, he taught at West Virginia State College and, later, at Howard University in Washington, D.C.

From there, Julian traveled to Vienna, Austria, where he studied for his doctoral degree and became interested in the medical use of soybeans. After returning to the United States, he created synthetic physostigmine, a drug used to treat glaucoma, a disease that results in blindness. When Dean

Blanchard, Julian's professor from DePauw University, heard of the discovery, he asked to have Julian appointed head of DePauw's chemistry department. In spite of his qualifications, Julian was rejected—again for racial reasons.

If the medical and educational communities were making race an issue, W. J. O'Brien of the Glidden Paint Company was not. He hired Julian as chief chemist and director of research at Glidden. This was a smart move. Julian's research took Glidden from a $35,000 loss to a profit of $135,000 in just one year.

During his lifetime, Julian owned more than one hundred chemical patents. He developed Aero-Foam, a substance that put out gas and oil fires and saved thousands of lives during World War II. His research on soybeans resulted in the manufacture of a synthetic hormone used in the treatment of cancer. He also developed a method of manufacturing cortisone, a drug that relieves arthritis pain.

In 1953, Julian founded Julian Laboratories, a pharmaceutical company. The first year his company made a mere $71.70. The second year he made $97,000. Six years later, he sold the company for $2,338,000.

As his scientific discoveries added up, Julian was honored with numerous awards and citations. His medical and scientific achievements were responsible for saving thousands of lives and reducing the suffering of millions of people—including some who had tried to keep him from accomplishing anything at all.

Ralph Bunche

Diplomat

1903–1971

I have deep-seated bias against hate and intolerance. I have a bias against racial and religious bigotry. I have a bias against war; a bias for peace. I have a bias which leads me to believe in the essential goodness in my fellow man; which leads me to believe that no problem of human relations is ever insoluble.

—Ralph Bunche

In 1950, the Nobel Peace Prize was awarded to an individual who temporarily brought an end to the bitter conflict between Jews and Arabs in the Middle East. The man who received the award was not an Arab or a Jew, but an African-American named Ralph Bunche.

Born in Detroit, Michigan, in 1904, Bunche and his family moved to Albuquerque, New Mexico, in 1915. Two years later his parents died, and his grandmother took young Ralph and his sister to Los Angeles. There he finished high school and enrolled at UCLA.

After graduating with highest honors, Bunche enrolled at Harvard University, where he earned a master's degree in government. While there, he met Percy Julian, the great chemist. Because of Julian's influence, Bunche was offered a position as director of the political science department at Howard University in Washington, D.C. He accepted it and went to work enthusiastically. Quickly discouraged by the segregation in Washington, he returned to Harvard, where he became the first African-American to earn a Ph.D. in political science.

In 1936, Bunche published *A World View of Race,* in which he states that racial prejudice exists partly because of economic needs. He writes, "The Negro was enslaved not because of his race but because there were very definite economic considerations which his enslavement served. The New World demanded his labor power. . . . But his race was soon used [as the reason for] the inhuman institution of slavery."

In 1944, Bunche went to work for the U.S. State Department, becoming the first African-American acting chief of the Division of Dependent Area Affairs. At the close of World War II, he was involved in establishing the United Nations (UN). In 1946, he joined the UN as director of the Division of Trusteeship and Non-Self-Governing Territories. This section worked to protect the rights of people still under colonial control. This became an area of great concern after the war as many nations in Africa, Asia, and the Middle East strove to become independent of European rule.

In 1950, Bunche received the Nobel Peace Prize for his work in bringing about a truce between warring Jews and Arabs in Palestine. Although fighting in the Middle East would break out again in the future, the truce was a major accomplishment. Not only did it bring temporary peace to the area, but it also showed that the newly created United Nations was capable of acting firmly to end the conflict.

In the following years, Bunche continued his diplomatic activities, working to end fighting in the Congo and on the island of Cyprus, supervising peace-keeping troops at Egypt's Suez Canal, and serving as a mediator in a dispute between India and Pakistan. In 1968, he became undersecretary of the UN, the highest rank ever held by an American.

Miles Davis
Jazz Musician, Trumpeter
1926–1991

John Coltrane
Jazz Musician, Saxophonist
1926–1967

Miles Davis

Jazz lovers mark 1926 as special—this is the year both Miles Davis and John Coltrane were born.

Miles Davis grew up in East St. Louis. His mother was a classically trained pianist, and perhaps it was from her that Davis inherited his love for music. He began playing the trumpet when he was thirteen and, after graduating from high school, he was invited to join the Billy Eckstine band. There he met Dizzy Gillespie and Charlie Parker. He soon moved to New York, where he spent many hours listening to the musicians at Minton's Playhouse. In 1947, Davis joined Charlie Parker's group and concentrated on developing his bebop style. In 1949, he and arranger Gil Evans released *Birth of the Cool*, which quickly became a jazz classic. Davis liked to work with different musicians in an effort to get just the right sound. He explored many jazz styles, including bebop, cool jazz, hard bop, modal jazz, and fusion (or electric) jazz. His willingness to constantly adapt his playing to accommodate new styles made him a leader in jazz music.

John Coltrane

John Coltrane was born in Hamlet, North Carolina. His father was a minister, and Coltrane grew up surrounded by church music. While in high school he experimented with various musical instruments and would practice for hours at a time. After graduation, he moved to Philadelphia to attend the Ornstein School of Music. He spent several years in the Navy, then returned to Philadelphia and began playing with various rhythm-and-blues groups. In 1955, he joined Miles Davis's quintet. He also worked with Thelonious Monk.

Coltrane suffered from drug and alcohol abuse, but in 1957, he turned to God and overcame his addictions. He studied musical styles from India and Africa, which he incorporated into his own work. In 1961, he formed his own quartet and created what many consider to be his finest music. In 1965, he was named Jazz Man of the Year by *Down Beat* magazine, and his record *A Love Supreme* (1964) was named Record of the Year. Coltrane's influence stems from his incredible skill and innovation. He and Davis helped make jazz one of the great American contributions to the world of music.

Lorraine Hansberry

Playwright
1930–1965

And because we are also, strangely enough under the circumstances, patriotic Americans, most of us . . . are still willing, despite the dogs and the hoses and the police, to set forth the message of our discontent by walking and talking.

—Lorraine Hansberry

When Lorraine Hansberry was twenty-six years old, she became the first African-American woman to have a play produced on Broadway and the youngest person to win the New York Drama Critics Circle Award for Best Play. Titled *A Raisin in the Sun,* the play is about an African-American family's efforts to move into an all-white neighborhood. This was a problem with which Hansberry was familiar.

When Hansberry was eight years old, her father, a successful Chicago businessman, moved their family into an all-white neighborhood. The reaction of the new neighbors was hostile. The Hansberrys were threatened, harassed, and finally evicted by court order. Mr. Hansberry, however, would not give up. With the help of lawyers from the NAACP, he challenged the lower court decision. Finally, in 1940, the Supreme Court ruled in his favor.

Meanwhile, Lorraine had become interested in the work of African-

American authors, particularly Langston Hughes. Graduating from high school in 1948, she enrolled at the University of Wisconsin, where she studied art and stage design. After completing her sophomore year, she moved to New York, where she met and married Robert Nemiroff, a music publisher.

During the next three years, Hansberry wrote her famous play *A Raisin in the Sun*. It was a wonderful play, but she had trouble getting it produced. Many producers felt there would be no interest in a serious black-oriented play. Besides, Hansberry was unknown, African-American, and a woman—three more strikes against her.

Determined to see her play performed on the stage, Hansberry set out to find investors. Eventually, she found people willing to take a chance. *A Raisin in the Sun* was an immediate hit. Booked into Broadway's Ethel Barrymore Theater on March 11, 1959, it ran for nineteen months and was made into a movie that won the Cannes Film Festival Award in 1961. A musical version won the Tony Award in 1974. The play itself has been translated into thirty languages.

The success of *A Raisin in the Sun* made Hansberry a celebrity. She was asked to comment on major political issues, especially as they related to women's rights and the growing Civil Rights Movement. In 1964, she wrote the text for a book called *The Movement*, a collection of photographs documenting the Civil Rights Movement. Her second play, *The Sign in Sidney Brustein's Window*, also opened that year.

In 1963, Hansberry was diagnosed with cancer, and it became increasingly difficult for her to write. She was in and out of hospitals until she died on January 12, 1965. Fragments from her plays, letters, and stories were collected by Robert Nemiroff in a book called *To Be Young, Gifted, and Black*. In it, Hansberry's strength, pride, humor, kindness, and love of life shine through. "I wish to live," she writes, "because life has within it that which is good, that which is beautiful and that which is love."

James Baldwin

Writer

1924—1987

I must oppose any attempt that Negroes may make to do to others what has been done to them. . . . I know the spiritual wasteland to which that road leads.

—James Baldwin

"And God gave Noah the rainbow sign. No more water, the fire next time!" These lines from a Negro spiritual gave James Baldwin the title for one of his most famous books, *The Fire Next Time.* That Baldwin should draw on a religious song for inspiration is not surprising, since he began preaching at age fourteen.

Born in Harlem in 1924, Baldwin was small, and other children often teased him about his looks. Feeling unloved and ugly, he would spend hours by himself in the public library reading and writing plays, poetry, and short stories.

In 1938, Baldwin entered DeWitt Clinton High School in Bronx, New York, where he became editor of the school newspaper. For the first time, he found friends who also enjoyed reading and writing. But his new friends were white and Jewish—people his father did not approve of and would not allow in his house. Resentful of his father and unable to cope with mounting family problems, Baldwin left home at age seventeen and began working on his first novel, *Go Tell It on the Mountain.*

In 1944, Baldwin met Richard Wright, the famous African-American novelist. With Wright's help, Baldwin obtained a Eugene Saxon Memorial Trust Award, which enabled him to continue his writing. In 1948, his first short story, "Previous Condition," was published, although he still had not been able to complete his novel.

Torn between his loyalty to the African-American community and his white friends, who could not understand the tension he felt as an African-American man living in a racist society, Baldwin moved to Paris. Soon, money became a major problem. Hungry and broke, Baldwin was forced to sell some of his clothes and even his typewriter. Living in France provided a healthy environment for his writing, however. The French did not reject him because of his color. Nor did they sneer at his desire to write. This enabled him to do what he could not do in the United States—creatively use his past and experience instead of trying to escape from them.

In 1949, Baldwin's essay "Everybody's Protest Novel" was published. The publication of this essay destroyed his friendship with Richard Wright, who felt the book criticized him. Suffering a nervous breakdown, Baldwin went to Switzerland to recover. There he finally completed *Go Tell It on the Mountain,* which was published in 1953.

After four years in Europe, Baldwin returned to the United States and sold his novel. A year later, he returned to Europe to work on a second book, *Another Country,* and a play called *The Amen Corner.* Unable to finish either to his satisfaction, he put both aside and wrote what would become his favorite novel, *Giovanni's Room* (1956).

Becoming increasingly preoccupied with the growing Civil Rights Movement in the United States, Baldwin returned to his native country. There he began to take part in sit-ins and allowed the movement to use his name for raising money. In 1955, the vicious murder in Mississippi of a fourteen-year-old African-American youth named Emmett Till had a strong impact on Baldwin. He was also affected by a trip with civil-rights leader Medgar Evers to investigate the murder of an African-American man by a white storekeeper. These experiences became the driving force behind his play *Blues for Mister Charlie* (1964).

As a result of his powerful books, Baldwin became known as a novelist and essayist. Angry, yet somehow hopeful, his essays, like his novels and plays, often focused on what he saw as the continuing, intertwining destinies of blacks and whites in America: "[W]e, the black and white, deeply need each other here if we are really to become a nation . . . if we are really, that is, to achieve our identity, our maturity, as men and women."

Wilma Rudolph

Olympic Track and Field Athlete
1940—1994

To this day, black women athletes are on the bottom of the ladder. White women [athletes] . . . make it on the front cover of magazines. The Wilma Rudolphs don't. That's my challenge.

—Wilma Rudolph

Born in St. Bethlehem, Tennessee, Wilma Rudolph was the seventeenth of nineteen children. Weighing a slight 4 pounds, 8 ounces (2 kg) at birth, Rudolph struggled to survive as one illness after another kept her weak and bedridden. Then, at age four, she was crippled by polio. Doctors said she would never walk again.

Rudolph's parents refused to accept her disability. They devoted their time and what little money they earned as a store clerk and a maid to help their daughter. The entire family took turns massaging and exercising Rudolph's leg. Each week, Rudolph's mother took her to a clinic 90 miles (145 km) away for heat and water treatments. After a year of therapy, there was some improvement.

By the time Rudolph was eight, she was walking with a leg brace. A short time later, she was fitted with a special high-topped shoe that enabled her to get along well enough to go to school. Although she walked with a limp, she never allowed her disability to hold her back. She played basketball with her brothers in the backyard. Often, she played by herself long after they had quit for the day.

Rudolph amazed everyone. One day, when she was eleven, she began playing basketball in her bare feet. Purposely, she had tossed aside her special shoe, confident that she could walk like everyone else. Within a few years, she was not only walking but also running—faster than many kids her own age. By the time Rudolph was fifteen, she had become an all-state high school basketball champion. In her sophomore year, she broke the girl's state basketball record, scoring 803 points in 25 games. Her track and field record was even more remarkable.

In her final year of high school, Rudolph qualified for the 1956 Olympics to be held in Melbourne, Australia. There she competed as a member of the U.S. 400-meter relay team and returned home with a bronze medal. The next year, she attended Tennessee State, where she excelled in track. In 1960, she qualified for the Summer Olympics in Rome and became the first American woman to win three gold medals in track—for the 100-meter dash, the 200-meter dash, and the 400-meter relay. As a result, she was voted U.S. Female Athlete of the Year by the Associated Press and dubbed the "World's Fastest Woman."

After graduating from college, Rudolph married and became a teacher. Eventually, she held jobs as a television host, speaker, and coach. Her determination and perseverance allowed her to accomplish what no other American female athlete had been able to do. Rudolph died in 1994.

Rosa Parks

Civil Rights Activist

1913—

I'm just an average citizen. Many black people before me were arrested for defying bus laws. They prepared the way.

—Rosa Parks

Shortly after 5:00 P.M. on Thursday, December 1, 1955, Rosa Parks finished her work as a seamstress at a local department store in Montgomery, Alabama, and boarded a bus. What began as an ordinary bus ride home became the event that sparked the Civil Rights Movement of the 1950s and 1960s.

Rosa McCauley Parks was born in Tuskegee, Alabama, in 1913 and grew up on a small farm with her brother, mother, and grandparents. She attended an all-black school that closed three months earlier than white schools so that the children could work in the fields.

When Parks turned eleven, her mother had saved enough money to send her to a private school in Montgomery. She attended high school until her mother became ill. After quitting school, she found a job as a house servant and began sending money back to her family in Tuskegee. When she married Raymond Parks in 1932, she returned to high school and graduated.

In 1943, Parks joined the NAACP and worked to ensure voting rights for African-Americans. She continued to work for the NAACP while holding various jobs as a housecleaner, seamstress, and office clerk. On the evening of December 1, 1955, while returning home from work, Parks boarded a bus and sat down. According to Montgomery law, African-Americans were required to sit in the back of the bus and give up their seats to white passengers as the bus filled. When Parks was asked to give up her seat to a white passenger on this particular evening, however, she refused. Immediately, the driver stopped the bus and called two policemen. Parks was arrested and taken to jail for violating the city ordinance.

Edgar Daniel Nixon, head of the NAACP in Montgomery, posted a $100 bond to get Parks released. He then called a meeting of African-American leaders to determine what action they should take. The meeting was held in the basement of the Dexter Avenue Baptist Church, where a young man named Martin Luther King, Jr., had just been appointed minister. By the end of the long evening, the leaders agreed to call a one-day boycott of all city buses for Monday, December 5. Although Parks was not the first person to be arrested for refusing to give up her seat on a bus, Nixon decided that she would be the last.

Over the weekend, thousands of leaflets announcing the boycott were printed and distributed. On Monday morning, the first buses began their run through the African-American neighborhoods. They finished the same way they began—empty. There were no black passengers. The boycott was a success. Immediately, organizers voted to continue it. They set up the Montgomery Improvement Association (MIA) and named Martin Luther King, Jr., its leader.

Meanwhile, Parks went to court. She was charged with violating a 1947 segregation statute. The judge found her guilty and fined her $10 plus $4 in court costs. The NAACP appealed the case to the U.S. Supreme Court.

While the boycott continued, the Ku Klux Klan and the White Citizens Council took action. They threatened the MIA organizers and harassed

African-Americans on the street. Hundreds of leaders and supporters, including Parks, were arrested. Many lost their jobs, and King's house was dynamited. Still the boycott continued.

People walked. They rode bicycles, caught cabs, and joined car pools. They drove wagons, hitchhiked, rode mules, and then walked some more. One elderly woman declared, "My feets is tired, but my soul is rested."

After 381 days of boycotting, the U.S. Supreme Court ruled in favor of Parks and declared Alabama laws on bus segregation unconstitutional. In April 1956, the bus company, which had lost more than $750,000 during the long boycott, agreed to integrate seating on its buses and hire African-American drivers. This was the first major step in a decades-long fight for civil rights in America.

Alex Palmer Haley

Writer

1921–1992

Born in Ithaca, New York, Alex Palmer Haley grew up in Henning, Tennessee, in a family where telling stories about kinfolk was a common way to pass the time. Some of these stories, which reached back to Africa, would one day provide the basis for *Roots,* Haley's most famous work.

Haley was already in the Coast Guard when World War II broke out. During the hundreds of hours he spent aboard ship, Haley began writing stories and eventually developed into an experienced, compelling writer. After leaving the Coast Guard, he moved to New York and began writing for magazines such as *Harpers* and *Reader's Digest.* He also wrote up an interview with jazz musician Miles Davis that appeared in *Playboy* magazine. Enormously successful, this article was the beginning of *Playboy's* popular interview series.

A second interview with Malcolm X led to Haley's first major success: a collaboration that resulted in the best-selling *Autobiography of Malcolm X.* Published in 1965, the book sold more than five million copies. Haley then began his research on *Roots,* a history of his own family, beginning with an African man named Kunta Kinte who was sold into slavery after being kidnapped from his home in the Gambia. *Roots* would later sell more than eight million copies and win almost three hundred different awards, including the National Book Award for 1976 and a "special citation" Pulitzer Prize in 1977. *Roots* was also made into a 12-hour miniseries that made television history.

Haley's work caused thousands of African-Americans to wonder about their backgrounds, and many attempted to trace their ancestors as Haley had done. Millions of white Americans gained a better understanding of the cruelties of slavery. *Roots* was meant as the story of one man's family, but for many people, it became the story of all African-Americans.

Ella Josephine Baker

Civil Rights Activist

1903–1986

Strong people don't need strong leaders.

—Ella Josephine Baker

Ella Josephine Baker was born in Norfolk, Virginia, and grew up in Littleton, North Carolina. Her parents stressed the importance of self-help, economic self-sufficiency, and racial pride.

After graduating from Shaw University in 1927, Baker moved to New York City. She was appalled at the poverty, hunger, and misery she saw in Harlem and became determined to do something about it. She joined the Young Negroes Cooperative League, whose goal was to achieve economic strength through consumer buying clubs and cooperative grocery stores. She also began working for a government program that promoted literacy among poor and immigrant workers. Though she worked with various women's groups, Baker refused to allow others to limit her to "women's issues."

In 1940, Baker became a field director for the National Association for the Advancement of Colored People (NAACP), the leading civil rights organization of the twentieth century. The NAACP's reliance on legal tactics, such as lawsuits to fight discrimination, frustrated Baker, who preferred mass participation campaigns such as marches. In 1946, she gave up her staff job with the organization, although she continued to work with it as president of its New York branch.

In 1958, Baker moved to Atlanta, Georgia, to coordinate a voter registration campaign being launched by the Southern Christian Leadership Conference (SCLC). The leaders of the group were men who believed in a highly structured organization. Baker preferred a looser, less-centralized approach. When a student-led sit-in campaign began in Greensboro, North Carolina, Baker left the SCLC to work with the student activists. She organized a conference of youthful sit-in leaders at Shaw University, and this led to the formation of the Student Nonviolent Coordinating Committee (SNCC—pronounced "snick"). SNCC quickly became a leading civil-rights organization. Working in rural areas to increase African-American voter registration, its student volunteers were frequently the target of Ku Klux Klan attacks—but they got results.

In 1964, Baker helped establish the Mississippi Freedom Democratic Party, which challenged the all-white Mississippi delegation at the Democratic National Convention in Atlantic City, New Jersey. Although they were not seated at the convention, the new party's demands forced the Democratic Party to change its rules for future delegates.

Baker is sometimes overlooked as a civil rights leader, although her impact was decisive and far reaching. Her faith in ordinary people was well justified, because it was ordinary people marching, protesting, voting, and demonstrating that made the Civil Rights Movement a success and changed U.S. history.

Thurgood Marshall

Supreme Court Justice
1908–1993

The United States Supreme Court stands at First and East Capital Streets, N.E., in Washington, D.C. Etched into the stone over its entrance are the words, "Equal Justice Under Law." For many years, those words were only scratches on a wall as far as African-Americans were concerned. But to Thurgood Marshall, the man who would one day become the first African-American Supreme Court justice, they were a promise and a commitment.

Marshall was born in Baltimore, Maryland, in 1908. As a boy, he often got into trouble at school. As punishment, the principal sent him to the school basement to memorize sections of the Constitution. This did not keep Marshall out of trouble, but it did help him later when he argued cases before the court.

After graduating with honors from Lincoln University in Pennsylvania, Marshall went to Howard University Law School in Washington, D.C. Finishing in 1933, he entered private practice, specializing in civil rights cases. In 1936, he began working for the NAACP, becoming head of its legal staff in 1938. One of the cases Marshall argued was that of Lloyd Lionel Gaines, a student whose request for admission to the all-white University of Missouri had been denied because of his race.

In 1896, the Supreme Court had ruled in the case of *Plessy v. Ferguson* that it was legal for a state government to maintain separate, or segregated, facilities for blacks and whites, provided the facilities were "equal." The "separate but equal" doctrine set forth in *Plessy v. Ferguson* originally referred to railroad cars, but later it included schools and other facilities.

Once a ruling has been handed down by the Supreme Court, it becomes very difficult to overturn. This is because people cannot be expected to know what the law is if the court keeps changing its mind. When the Supreme Court hands down a ruling, it establishes what is called a precedent. Lawyers and judges refer to the court's past rulings (precedents) to determine how the law should be interpreted in new cases.

In arguing the Gaines case, Marshall pointed out that "equal" did not exist in this situation. Because there was no separate law school for African-Americans at the University of Missouri, the Supreme Court ruled that the university would have to either admit Gaines or give him an opportunity to attend a comparable school in the state. The Gaines case established an important precedent: for segregation to be allowable, it must be equal. The question then became, what is equal?

This issue came up in another of Marshall's cases, *Sweatt v. Painter,* in 1950. Herman Sweatt had been denied entrance to the all-white University of Texas Law School in 1946. When he sued, the Texas courts gave the state six months to set up a separate African-American law school. Marshall persuaded the Supreme Court that a hastily set-up, makeshift law school could not provide an education equivalent to that provided by the university. As a result, the court ordered that Sweatt be admitted.

By 1954, Marshall was ready to challenge segregation itself. The case was *Brown v. Board of Education,* involving the board of education of Topeka, Kansas. Drawing partly on psychological studies, Marshall convinced the court that segregated education could never result in equal education. Segregated black children concluded that they were not as good as white children. Segregation automatically implied inferiority, argued Marshall, and automatically placed African-American children at a disadvantage. The court unanimously agreed.

Unfortunately, Marshall's victory did not result in immediate desegregation. The Supreme Court had ordered the states to integrate their schools "with all deliberate speed." In many areas, this meant no speed at all. Prince Edward County in Virginia closed its schools for five years rather than integrate them. Marshall and his staff persisted, filing case after case to force individual school districts to obey the Supreme Court's ruling.

School desegregation was not Marshall's only concern. As chief counsel for the NAACP, and later as director-counsel for its Legal and Educational Fund, he directed and coordinated legal attacks on discrimination in voting, housing, restaurants and other public places, buses, and criminal procedure. He traveled thousands of miles interviewing witnesses, locating evidence, and arguing cases.

Of the 32 major cases he argued for the NAACP, Marshall won 29. His record as judge on the U.S. Court of Appeals for the Second Circuit, to which he was appointed in 1962, was equally impressive. Of the more than 150 opinions he handed down, none was reversed by a higher court. In 1965, President Lyndon Johnson appointed Marshall solicitor general of the Department of Justice. Of the nineteen cases he argued for the government, he won fourteen.

When President Johnson appointed Marshall associate justice of the Supreme Court in 1967, he became the first African-American man to serve in this position. It was an appropriate distinction for a man who had done so much to translate the words "Equal Justice Under Law" into reality.

On June 27, 1991, eighty-two-year-old Marshall resigned from the Supreme Court due to failing health. He died in 1993.

The Little Rock Nine

On the morning of September 4, 1957, fifteen-year-old Elizabeth Eckford arrived at school and was met by a National Guardsman armed with a bayonet. Barred from entering the school, she turned around and, with a taunting mob at her heels, walked 100 yards, alone, to a bus stop. The school year at Central High School in Little Rock, Arkansas, had begun. (See "Elizabeth Eckford's Account of Day One at Central High School.")

Three years earlier, in 1954, the U.S. Supreme Court had ruled in *Brown v. Board of Education* that black and white children must be allowed to attend school together. The court's decision reversed its earlier ruling that "separate but equal" schools were legal. Thurgood Marshall had presented the legal argument for Brown, pointing out that African-American schools were not equal. They lacked adequate money, books, and basic materials, and were often in poor physical condition. He argued further that keeping black and white children apart was itself wrong and discriminatory.

When the Little Rock schools failed to follow the court's ruling, the NAACP decided to take action. It selected nine African-American students, including Eckford, from a group of more than eighty applicants to integrate Central High School in Little Rock. Several weeks after Elizabeth Eckford's experience, the nine students, armed with a federal court order, tried to attend classes. Four hours later, they were taken home as hundreds of screaming segregationists roamed the streets outside the school. The next day, the nine students stayed home. However, on September 25, they finally attended classes under the protection of the U.S. Army's 101st Airborne Division.

For the rest of that year, the Little Rock Nine, as they were called, attended class under military escort. They learned algebra, biology, English, and chemistry—but they made history themselves.

Medgar Evers

Civil Rights Leader
1925–1963

If I die, it will be in a good cause. I've been fighting for America just as much as the soldiers in Vietnam.

—Medgar Evers

In 1955, the name of Medgar Evers topped a nine-man death list. The list was shortened to eight when the Reverend George T. Lee was gunned down in Belzoni, Mississippi. Then, on June 12, 1963, Evers was killed, shot in the back as he returned home from a meeting in Jackson, Mississippi. As far as the murderers were concerned, both Evers and Lee were guilty of the same crime: they were encouraging African-Americans to exercise their right to vote.

Born near Decatur, Mississippi, Evers was the third of four children. At one time he had to walk 12 miles (19 km) each way to get to school, but Evers was determined to get an education. After his discharge from the army, he returned to Mississippi and enrolled at Alcorn A & M College. He graduated in 1952 and joined the NAACP. Because of his leadership abilities, Evers was appointed field secretary after only two years.

At that time, segregation in most public places was still in effect. Evers worked hard to end it. He made speeches, led demonstrations, and encouraged

African-Americans to boycott stores owned by white businessmen who refused to hire or promote African-American workers. Although Evers knew his work was dangerous, he refused to quit.

When Evers was killed, demonstrations and rallies occurred nationwide, and African-American voter registration increased. Pressured by the unrest, President John F. Kennedy requested passage of a new civil rights act outlawing racial segregation in public places. A white racist named Byron de la Beckwith was charged with Evers's murder and tried twice, in 1963 and 1964. Both times, all-white juries could not reach a decision, and Beckwith was released. He was finally convicted in 1994.

Although some people think voting is a waste of time, Evers knew better. Because of people like him, African-American men and women now hold political office, and segregation in public places is against the law in the United States.

Sit-Ins

"I sat-in at a restaurant for six months, and when they finally agreed to serve me, they didn't have what I wanted," went a famous line. In reality, the sit-in movement was no joke. It began in Greensboro, North Carolina, at 4:30 P.M. on the afternoon of February 1, 1960. On that day, Ezell Blair Jr., Joseph McNeil, David Richmond, and Franklin McCain entered an F.W. Woolworth store. They sat down at a segregated lunch counter, ordered coffee, and then refused to leave when told, "We don't serve Negroes."

The four young men had expected not to be served. What no one had expected, however, was that they would sit there and politely, but firmly, refuse to leave. This was 1960, and throughout the South, African-Americans were not allowed to sit at the same lunch counters, swim at the same beaches, use the same water fountains, or worship at the same churches as white people.

The next day, the four men returned to Woolworth's, this time accompanied by sixteen other students. Again they sat at the lunch counter, requested service, and were refused. Again they declined to leave. On Wednesday, February 3, seventy students filled the Woolworth's store. This time, the group included white students as well as black. Many brought school books and studied while they waited. By this time, their protest had become known nationwide as a "sit-in."

On Thursday, there was trouble. An angry group of white teenagers began shoving and cursing the protestors but were quickly removed by the police. By February 10, the sit-in movement had spread to five other states.

By September 1961, more than 70,000 people, both black and white, had participated in sit-ins at segregated restaurants and lunch counters, kneel-ins at segregated churches, read-ins at segregated libraries, and swim-ins at pools and beaches. Over 3,600 people had been arrested, and more than 100 students had been expelled. But they were getting results. Many places did agree to integrate. On June 10, 1964, the U.S. Senate passed a major civil rights bill outlawing racial discrimination in all public places. President Lyndon Johnson signed it on July 2. But the highest credit still goes to the four brave students from North Carolina who first sat-in and waited it out.

Freedom Riders

"I'm taking a trip on the Greyhound Bus line. I'm riding up front, into Jackson this time." These were the lyrics, but the opening beat was provided by thirteen Freedom Riders (seven black and six white) who went on the road May 4, 1961, to desegregate southern bus terminals.

Although the Supreme Court had ruled in 1946 and 1960 that segregation was illegal on interstate buses, segregation prevailed in much of the South. At bus stations, African-Americans were forced to use separate waiting rooms, restrooms, and ticket counters. Black passengers were allowed to sit

Freedom Riders sit outside their burned bus in Anniston, Alabama.

only at the back of buses. If all the seats in the back were taken, they had to stand, even if there were empty seats in the front. To fight this injustice, the Congress of Racial Equality (CORE), a civil rights group under the direction of James Farmer, began the "Freedom Rides."

The first group of Freedom Riders traveled peacefully through Virginia and North Carolina. In South Carolina, two members of their party were attacked, but the group continued its journey. In Georgia, things were quiet. In Anniston, Alabama, a mob shot out the tires of one bus, broke a window, and tossed a firebomb inside. The bus went up in flames, and the Freedom Riders barely got out alive. The second bus made it into Birmingham. There, Police Commissioner Eugene "Bull" Connor, a segregationist, told city police officers to take 15 minutes to "visit their mothers" (it was Mother's Day), leaving the Freedom Riders unprotected. The Riders were attacked by Ku Klux Klan thugs and beaten viciously. James Peck, a white CORE member, required fifty-six stitches after his head was bashed in with lead pipes.

After the attack at Anniston, CORE members were joined by young people from the Student Nonviolent Coordinating Committee (SNCC), another civil rights group. Together they rode into Montgomery, Alabama, where Martin Luther King, Jr., was to address them at a mass rally at the First Baptist Church. Again rioters attacked and, when the local police failed to protect the group, U.S. Attorney General Robert F. Kennedy sent in six hundred U.S. Marshals to restore order.

That night, twelve hundred African-Americans gathered at the church. An angry mob showed up, but marshals stepped in, and the mob backed down. Meanwhile, Governor Patterson declared martial law and ordered the Alabama National Guard under General Henry Graham to the church. Patterson called Kennedy and told him that General Graham could not guarantee King's safety. "Have the general call me," said Kennedy angrily. "I want him to say it to me. I want to hear a general of the U.S. Army say he can't protect Martin Luther King." Of course, General Graham had said no such thing, and the National Guard finally dispersed the mob and led King and the others to safety.

In the months that followed, there were more Freedom Rides and hundreds of arrests—350 in Jackson, Mississippi, alone. Hundreds were thrown in jail after being charged with disorderly conduct, disturbing the peace, and trespassing. Still, they kept coming. Segregation on buses was finally brought to an end.

Fannie Lou Hamer

Civil Rights Leader
1917–1977

I'm sick and tired of being sick and tired.

—Fannie Lou Hamer

"You can pray until you faint, but if you don't get up and try to do something, God is not gonna put it in your lap." So spoke Fannie Lou Hamer at a 1964 meeting in Indianola, Mississippi, where she urged African-Americans to register to vote. It was dangerous work; a year earlier, she had been beaten up for doing it.

Born October 6, 1917, in Mississippi, Hamer was the youngest of twenty children. Her parents were sharecroppers. Sharecropping is a system whereby people work the land and share the profits on the crops. It's a hard way to make a living, and sharecroppers generally are born poor, live poor, and die poor.

At age six, Hamer began helping in the cotton fields. At twelve, she was forced to drop out of school and work full-time to help support her family. Once grown, she married another sharecropper named Perry "Pap" Hamer.

In 1962, Hamer and seventeen other African-Americans took a bus to the courthouse to register to vote. On their return home, police stopped their bus, saying it was "painted the wrong color." Hamer and the others were arrested.

After Hamer was released from jail, the owner of the plantation where Hamer worked told her that if she insisted on voting, she would have to get off his land. Hamer refused to back down and was forced to leave the plantation that same day. That evening, night riders fired sixteen bullets into the home of the woman with whom Hamer had gone to stay. Still, Hamer would not give up. "We're tired of all this beating," she said. "It's been a hundred years and we're still being beaten and shot at. Crosses are still being burned because we want to vote. But I'm going to stay in Mississippi, and if they shoot me down, I'll be buried here."

By this time, Hamer had begun working on welfare and voter registration programs for two civil rights organizations, the Southern Christian Leadership Conference and the Student Nonviolent Coordinating Committee. To focus greater national attention on voter discrimination, civil rights groups created the Mississippi Freedom Democratic Party (MFDP). The MFDP sent a delegation, which included Hamer, to Atlantic City, where the Democratic Party was holding its national convention for the 1964 presidential nomination. The MFDP's purpose was to challenge the regular all-white Mississippi delegation on the grounds that it did not fairly represent all the people of Mississippi.

Convention-goers reached a compromise that gave voting and speaking rights to two delegates from the MFDP and seated the rest as honored guests. The Democrats agreed that in the future, no delegation would be allowed from a state where anyone was illegally denied the right to vote. A year later, President Johnson pushed through Congress a voting rights bill that protected African-American voters.

Hamer continued to work on equal rights and antipoverty programs in her later years. Speaking of discrimination, she once said, "This ain't just Mississippi's problem. It's America's problem." Thanks to Hamer, America has less of a problem today.

Malcolm X

Black Power Leader
1925–1965

We have to keep in mind at all times that we are not fighting for integration, nor are we fighting for separation. We are fighting for recognition as free humans in this society.

—Malcolm X

He was born Malcolm Little; as a young man he was called Detroit Red; but the world remembers him as Malcolm X. Born in Omaha, Nebraska, he was the seventh of eleven children. His father, Reverend Earl Little, was a Baptist minister and a strong believer in Marcus Garvey's ideas of African-American independence and self-respect. These ideas did not sit well with the local Ku Klux Klan. As a result, after Malcolm's birth, the family moved, first to Milwaukee, Wisconsin, and later to Lansing, Michigan.

Unfortunately, Reverend Little's ideas were no more popular in Lansing than they had been in Omaha and, in 1929, members of a local vigilante group set fire to the Littles' home. Malcolm's father was not one to be bullied, however. He stayed and built another home. But when Malcolm was six, his father was killed, possibly murdered.

Things were never the same for Malcolm after that. He quit school after the eighth grade. He traveled first to Boston, Massachusetts, and then to Harlem, New York, where he became involved in crime. In 1946, at the age of twenty-one, he was charged with burglary and sent to prison for six and a half years. While in prison, Malcolm became interested in the Nation of Islam, popularly known as the Black Muslims. This religious group, led by Elijah Muhammad, promoted African-American economic independence and sought to establish a separate African-American state either in the United States or in Africa.

Malcolm joined the Black Muslims. According to custom, he dropped his original last name and called himself Malcolm X. Serious about his new religion, he studied its teachings with interest. He also began educating himself by reading the encyclopedia and memorizing words from the dictionary.

Malcolm X was released from prison in 1952, he became a Muslim minister and spent the next twelve years organizing mosques and spreading the Black Muslim message. He condemned the nonviolent attempts of other African-American leaders to achieve integration, saying, "You can't stick a knife in a man's back nine inches and then pull it out six inches and say you're making progress." Many people were attracted by Malcolm X's ideas and supported him when he condemned the seemingly slow progress of the Civil Rights Movement.

Malcolm X's success as a speaker and organizer caused jealousy and resentment. In December 1963, Elijah Muhammad suspended him from the religious group. Three months later, Malcolm X quit the Nation of Islam and organized his own group, called the Organization of Afro-American Unity (OAAU).

In the summer of 1964, Malcolm X traveled to the Middle East and Africa to see how the Muslim religion was practiced there. Impressed, he converted to orthodox Islam and returned to the United States, denouncing Elijah Muhammad as a religious fake and a racist.

The Black Muslim newspaper, *Muhammad Speaks*, responded by calling Malcolm X a liar and saying he was "worthy of death." The threat was not an idle one. On February 14, 1965, his home was firebombed—just as his father's home had been bombed thirty-six years before. One week later, on February 21, Malcolm X was shot to death at a rally in the Audubon Ballroom in New York. Three Black Muslims were convicted of the murder, but the Nation of Islam officially denied having anything to do with his killing.

Malcolm X's death came as a great shock. To thousands of black people around the world, he personified revolution. He was able to appeal to ordinary people and articulate the anger and frustration they felt. Above all, he symbolized unyielding defiance and resistance in the face of prejudice, discrimination, and repression.

The 1963 March
on Washington

They came by car, and they came by plane—in two thousand chartered buses and thirty special trains, on foot, on bicycles, and in wheelchairs. It was August 28, 1963, and 250,000 people had gathered in Washington, D.C., to make the point that African-Americans were still not free.

The idea for the march had come from Bayard Rustin, close friend and adviser to A. Philip Randolph. Randolph felt that the sit-ins and protests being held throughout the South needed the backing of a massive, national

demonstration that would show a unified demand for civil and economic rights. Rustin suggested a march involving all the civil rights organizations to bring attention to the need for jobs, a higher minimum wage, a guaranteed income, and full rights for everyone.

Earlier, in June, President John F. Kennedy had announced on national television that he would submit a civil rights bill to Congress that would force owners of restaurants, hotels, theaters, and stores to serve any orderly person without regard to race. He opposed the Washington march, fearing it would create a backlash in Congress that would make his legislation harder to pass. But leaders of the March on Washington decided to forge ahead.

By 9:00 A.M., on the day of the march, forty thousand people were gathered at the base of the Washington Monument. An hour and a half later, more than ninety thousand people covered the grounds. Speakers began to address the crowd. Floyd McKissick delivered a speech for James Farmer of CORE, who was in a Louisiana jail because of his civil rights activities. John Lewis of SNCC spoke angrily of "[splintering] the segregated South into a thousand pieces." Roy Wilkins of the NAACP demanded passage of the civil rights bill. But it was the words of Dr. Martin Luther King, Jr., in his famous "I Have a Dream" speech, that echoed and re-echoed across the country.

Thousands who stood in the sweltering heat and listened to the words of freedom responded with hope, faith, and determination. The future would be rocked by riots, war, and assassinations, but on this day, 100 years and 274 days after the signing of the Emancipation Proclamation, thousands of American citizens stood together, reminding the nation and the world of what freedom really meant.

Roy Wilkins

Civil Rights Leader
1901–1981

In 1932, Roy Wilkins was asked by the NAACP to investigate reports of racial discrimination against African-Americans working on a federally financed flood control project in Mississippi. Wilkins agreed and, along with another NAACP worker, made his way south.

Arriving in Mississippi, the two men dressed in old clothes and got jobs as laborers on the flood project. Working undercover, they quietly gathered the information they needed. They had the look; they had the walk; they had the talk. Only one thing was wrong, and it could have gotten both of them killed. Wilkins's hands were long, graceful, and smooth—not the hands of a laborer. A white storekeeper noticed this and grew suspicious. By that time, however, Wilkins and his companion had enough information to convince Congress to take action, and they quickly left.

Wilkins was born in St. Louis, Missouri, on August 30, 1901. His mother died of tuberculosis when he was three years old. Together with his brother and sister, he was sent to live with an aunt and uncle in St. Paul, Minnesota. After graduating from high school, where he was editor of the school paper, Wilkins enrolled at the University of Minnesota. To help pay his tuition, he worked as a railroad porter, a waiter, and a clean-up man in the stockyards. He also edited the university newspaper and an African-American paper called the St. Paul *Appeal*. In his spare time, he served as secretary for the local branch of the NAACP.

After college, Wilkins went to work for the Kansas City *Call*, the city's leading African-American newspaper. For the first time, he found himself living in an area where there was widespread segregation. He responded by working harder for the NAACP and leading a successful campaign against the re-election of a pro-segregation senator. This work brought Wilkins to the attention of NAACP leaders and, in 1931, he was offered the job of assistant executive secretary. He was to remain an NAACP leader for forty-six years, becoming executive secretary in 1955.

During those years, the NAACP took legal action to overturn school segregation and encourage civil rights legislation. Wilkins played a major role in these activities, getting support for the 1964 Civil Rights Act, the 1965 Voting Rights Act, and the 1968 Fair Housing Act. He was a key organizer and supporter of the famous 1963 March on Washington. Under his leadership, the NAACP grew to include approximately 500,000 members with 1,700 chapters across the country. When thousands of protesters were arrested during the sit-ins, marches, and demonstrations of the 1950s and 1960s, the NAACP took the lead in providing bail money and legal and organizational support. Wilkins was one of those arrested.

Defending the willingness of protestors to engage in civil disobedience, Williams said, "We condemn the propaganda that Negro citizens must 'earn' their rights through good behavior. Good behavior . . . wins respect of our fellow citizens which we value and seek, but no American is required to 'earn' his rights as a citizen. His human rights come from God, and his citizenship rights come from the Constitution." These were rights Wilkins spent his lifetime trying to protect.

Alvin Ailey
1931–1989

Arthur Mitchell
1934–

Dancers, Choreographers

Alvin Ailey

Many people love to dance, but Alvin Ailey and Arthur Mitchell made dancing their life's work.

Alvin Ailey began studying dance after he graduated from high school and became the choreographer for the Lester Horton Theater. A choreographer's job is to design the dance. He or she decides the sequence of steps the dancers do, where they stand, and how the dance should look. This requires an extensive knowledge of dance techniques, as well as the ability to creatively combine dance steps to form a rhythmic, flowing pattern.

Born in Rogers, Texas, Ailey worked in the cotton fields next to his mother before they moved to Los Angeles. In 1954, Ailey moved to New York, where he was chosen as a dancer in the musical *House of Flowers*. In 1958, he established the Alvin Ailey American Dance Theater. Over the years, more than fifteen million people around the world saw his dancers perform. In addition to creating more than fifty dances for members of his

Arthur Mitchell

own dance troupe, he was a sought-after choreographer for other major dance groups.

Arthur Mitchell began his dance training in ballet. As the lead dancer with the New York City Ballet,

Alvin Ailey surrounded by other dancers in the 1960s

he was the first African-American featured in a major ballet company. For many years it was said that African-American dancers lacked the correct physique for ballet. Mitchell's wonderful performances did much to put that prejudice to rest. When Martin Luther King, Jr., was murdered in 1968, Mitchell decided to set up ballet classes for poor children in Harlem as a living tribute to him. Eventually, this became the Dance Theater of Harlem, which is now regarded as one of the premier dance companies in the world.

Martin Luther King, Jr.

Civil Rights Leader
1929–68

I have a dream that my four little children will one day live in a nation where they will not be judged by the color of their skin, but by the content of their character.

—Martin Luther King, Jr.

In 1954, Martin Luther King, Jr., became a pastor of the Dexter Avenue Baptist Church in Montgomery, Alabama. A year later, Rosa Parks was arrested for refusing to give up her bus seat for a white man. Her arrest marked the beginning of King's lifelong struggle in the Civil Rights Movement—a commitment that would bring him love, admiration, anger, and hate. It would demand his courage, faith, freedom and, eventually, his life.

King was born in Atlanta, Georgia, on January 15, 1929, and raised in a quiet, African-American middle-class neighborhood. His father, the pastor of Ebenezer Baptist Church in Atlanta, and his mother, a schoolteacher, were highly respected professionals in the African-American community.

King entered Morehouse College when he was only fifteen years old. After graduation, he became an ordained minister and enrolled at Crozer Theological Seminary in Chester, Pennsylvania, for a master's degree. There he studied the teachings of Mahatma Gandhi, the leader who struggled to gain

India's independence from England. King became convinced that nonviolent action was the best way to bring about change.

Later, while pursuing his doctorate at Boston University, King met and married Coretta Scott. In 1954, they traveled to Montgomery, where he became pastor of Dexter Avenue Baptist Church.

After Rosa Parks was arrested, King organized the successful Montgomery Bus Boycott. He persevered even after his house was firebombed in January 1956. To continue the desegregation movement, King helped form the Southern Christian Leadership Conference (SCLC) in February 1957 and was named its president. Guided by nonviolent philosophy and Christian beliefs, the SCLC was to become one of the dominant civil rights organizations in the South.

In 1958, King wrote his first book, *Stride Toward Freedom*. Two weeks after it was published, he was stabbed by a mentally ill African-American woman. When he recovered, he and Coretta visited India. Shortly after their return, the King family moved to Atlanta, where King joined his father as co-pastor of the Ebenezer Baptist Church.

In February 1960, the student sit-in movement got under way in Greensboro, North Carolina. Student leaders set up SNCC to guide the protests, and the SCLC, under King's leadership, offered its support. King also gave his support to CORE when it began its Freedom Rides to integrate interstate buses in 1961.

In April 1963, King launched a campaign to stop segregation in Birmingham, Alabama, one of the South's most violent and segregated cities. He demanded desegregation of lunch counters, restrooms, and drinking fountains, and the hiring of African-Americans by local businesses and the city government. After three days of demonstrations, the police, using dogs, moved against the protestors. King was arrested, jailed, and placed in solitary confinement. Eight white clergymen signed a statement denouncing the protests and urging Birmingham's black ministers to show restraint.

King was dismayed. As a man of God he had hoped for the support of the white clergy even though their churches were still segregated. From his jail cell he wrote a nine thousand-word appeal to his fellow ministers. This "Letter From Birmingham City Jail" became one of the most famous statements of the Civil Rights Movement. Thousands of copies were printed and read by people across the country. Shortly afterward, King was released, and many of the charges against him were dropped. But Birmingham had not yet changed its ways. Something dramatic was needed to capture the attention of the nation.

King scheduled a children's demonstration for Thursday, May 2. Hundreds of youngsters, ages six through sixteen, took part. Before the march was over, police had hauled 959 children off to jail. During the second day of the march, police, using powerful fire hoses, knocked children down with water while police dogs attacked them. Americans who witnessed the attacks on television were furious.

President John F. Kennedy immediately sent two officials from the Justice Department to negotiate a settlement. King had four demands: that all downtown stores be immediately desegregated; that African-Americans be hired as salespeople and clerks; that all demonstrators under arrest be released; and that a permanent biracial committee be set up. By the end of the week, city leaders gave in to all the demands.

Meanwhile, plans were being made for a march on Washington. Originally planned to build support for President Kennedy's civil rights bill, it became one of the turning points in the Civil Rights Movement. The triumphant gathering brought a climax—but not an end—to the movement. On December 10, 1964, King was awarded the Nobel Peace Prize for his efforts.

The 1964 Civil Rights Act ended segregation in public places, but did not deal with the problem of voting rights. Late in 1964, the SCLC was asked to come to Selma, Alabama, to take over a voter registration drive

SNCC had begun a year earlier. On January 18, 1965, King led the first demonstration to the county courthouse without any incidents. As the marches continued, however, state troopers became brutal. On February 18, a twenty-five-year-old African-American man named Jimmy Lee Jackson was killed when he tried to stop a state trooper from beating his mother.

In protest, another march took place in Selma. It resulted in a police riot when state troopers charged marchers attempting to cross the Edmund Pettus Bridge. More than 140 people were injured. In response, King invited clergy to Selma to join him on another march. Shortly after it ended, James Reeb, a white minister, was killed. As a result of the violence in Selma, Congress passed the 1965 Voting Rights Act, which guaranteed African-American suffrage. King decided it was time to take the movement north.

Deciding to concentrate on housing needs first, King moved into a rundown apartment in Chicago, Illinois. He then announced his plans to lead a rent strike if slum landlords did not upgrade their properties. He also set up Operation Breadbasket to promote African-American job opportunities. The drive to eliminate slums in Chicago resulted in promises and not much else. Operation Breadbasket was more successful. Faced with boycotts, a number of businesses either went out of business or agreed to hire African-Americans.

By 1965, national interest in civil rights had begun to fade as more people shifted their attention to the Vietnam War. President Johnson, who had once supported King, turned against him after King spoke out against the war. Many African-Americans, impatient with the slow progress of the Civil Rights Movement, were turning to violence.

But not everyone had lost faith in King. Sanitation workers in Memphis, Tennessee, asked for his help. Poor and mostly African-American, they had gone on strike in an effort to get the city to meet their demands. So far, they had been unsuccessful. They hoped that King's presence would make a difference. Over the next few weeks, King worked to organize a series of nonviolent demonstrations to support the sanitation workers' demands.

On the evening of April 4, 1968, King walked out on the balcony of his Memphis motel room and was shot dead by James Earl Ray. As news of his death flashed across television screens and newspapers, riots broke out in American cities. Over 100,000 people stood outside the Ebenezer Baptist Church in Atlanta, where King's funeral was held. Thousands of speeches were made in tribute to him, but it is King's own words that echo the loudest. In a sermon he delivered a few months before his death, he said,

> There is, deep down within all of us, an instinct—a "Drum Major" instinct, a desire to be out in front, a desire to lead the parade. . . . If any of you are around when I have to meet my day, I don't want a long funeral. And if you get somebody to deliver the eulogy, tell him not to talk too long. . . . I'd like somebody to mention on that day that Martin Luther King, Jr. . . . did try to feed the hungry . . . that I did try, in my life, to visit those who were in prison . . . that I tried to love and serve humanity. Yes, if you want to say that I was a Drum Major, say that I was a Drum Major for justice; say that I was a Drum Major for peace; that I was a Drum Major for righteousness.

The Black Power Movement

The Civil Rights Movement of the 1950s and 1960s was fueled by courage, determination, and the belief that the promises of American democracy would be made good someday. But violence and the resistance of white people to the movement unleashed anger, frustration, and resentment in the African-American community.

The development of African-American political power and the gradual appearance of African-American elected officials were a direct result of the voter registration campaigns of the Civil Rights Movement. It took years for these developments to become apparent, however. More rapid and visible progress was made in the desegregation of lunch counters, movie theaters, and other public places, but none of it came easily. As poverty and unemployment continued to gnaw at the African-American community, the Black Power Movement came into being.

Unlike the Civil Rights Movement, which was guided by a coalition of organizations such as CORE, SCLC, and the NAACP and directed toward definite goals, the Black Power Movement was a loosely drawn jumble of organizations and individuals united by their rejection of white society and their appeal to African-American pride and black consciousness.

Most notable of the groups identified with the Black Power Movement was the Black Panther Party. Begun in 1966, it soon included fifteen hundred members in thirty-eight chapters. Based primarily in the large cities of the North and West, it helped establish day-care centers and provide free breakfasts for poor people. Although its programs were not revolutionary, its rhetoric was. The bitter accusations of its leaders against whites in general, and the police in particular, resulted in hostility and bloodshed. A number of Panther members were involved in shoot-outs with the police. Two leaders were killed in Chicago when dozens of police shot up their apartment. The police claimed they shot in self-defense, but later evidence threw considerable doubt on that claim.

The Black Muslims, or Nation of Islam, a religious group that preached black self-respect, was also identified with the Black Power Movement, thanks to Malcolm X, its most eloquent spokesman. His murder by fellow Muslims in 1965 cost the Nation of Islam much of its appeal, however.

Olympic gold medalist Tommie Smith raises his fist in the Black Power salute in 1968.

Another group involved in the Black Power Movement was the Student Nonviolent Coordinating Committee (SNCC), the student organization that had been created to help guide the sit-ins. By the late 1960s, some of SNCC's leaders, particularly Stokely Carmichael, refused to work any longer with whites.

All these groups, though different in many ways, were similar in their antiwhite statements and rejection of Martin Luther King, Jr.'s nonviolent philosophy. It was a rejection that King found painful. Also upsetting to King were the riots that broke out in over a hundred American cities in the late 1960s. The first took place in Watts in Los Angeles in 1965. Before it was over, 34 people were dead, 898 were injured, and 4,000 had been arrested. It set a pattern that was to be repeated in the long, hot summers ahead.

The riots shocked and frightened the nation by revealing a depth of African-American resentment that went beyond criminals and radicals. Many widely respected blacks showed the same resentment. Heavyweight champion Muhammad Ali made his feelings plain when he refused to fight in Vietnam, saying, "No Vietcong ever called me Nigger." Olympic medalists Tommie Smith and John Carlos raised their fists in the Black Power salute as they were about to receive their medals in 1968. Black people across the country began wearing African clothes and "natural" hairstyles to express their pride. The slogans "Black Power" and "Black Is Beautiful" were heard everywhere.

Although the Black Power Movement was attacked by those who felt it destroyed white support for civil rights, it played a part in pressuring President Lyndon Johnson to declare a "War on Poverty." During his administration, dozens of programs were established to promote better health, education, jobs, and housing for poor people, many of them African-American. Although some of the programs failed, many were successful.

Marian Wright Edelman

Children's Advocate

1939—

One dollar up front saves many dollars down the road.

—Slogan of the Children's Defense Fund

African-American children were not allowed to play in the city parks in Bennesttsville, South Carolina, so Marian Wright Edelman's father created a playground for them behind the church where he was minister. His daughter learned from his example. When she grew up, she established an organization that helps children all over the United States.

After graduating from high school, Edelman entered Spelman College in Atlanta, Georgia. During her junior year, she traveled to France and Switzerland. When she returned to the United States, she joined the fight to end segregation. She began by participating in a sit-in and was arrested.

In 1963, Edelman went to Mississippi to help with the voter registration campaign. After graduating from Yale Law School, she became the first African-American woman to practice law in Mississippi. She began working for the NAACP Legal Defense and Educational Fund in Mississippi, representing civil rights demonstrators and working on school desegregation lawsuits. She also became involved with Mississippi's Head Start program, which aimed to provide better education for young children. During this time, she met her future husband, Peter Edelman, who was a member of Senator Robert Kennedy's staff.

In 1968, Marian Edelman moved to Washington, D.C., to provide legal assistance to the Poor People's Campaign, an effort by the civil rights leadership to highlight the problems of the poor. She also began the Washington Research Project to identify how well laws aimed at helping poor people really worked. The project soon became the Children's Defense Fund (CDF), an organization dedicated to helping and protecting children across the country. During this time, Edelman became the first African-American woman to serve on the board of directors of Yale University. Not to be outdone, Yale's rival, Harvard University, hired Edelman to direct its Center for Law and Education. But Edelman's first concern was the Children's Defense Fund. In 1973, she became its president and, in 1979, she returned to Washington to work for it full-time.

The Children's Defense Fund aims to guarantee every child a "Healthy Start, a Head Start, a Fair Start, a Safe Start, and a Moral Start." It encourages the passage of laws that will provide children with health care, education, economic security, and protection from abuse and neglect. Edelman's work with CDF earned her a Presidential Medal of Freedom in 2000.

Edelman has written several books, including one for young people called *Stand for Children*. This title represents the philosophy of a woman who has been standing up for children all her life.

Maya Angelou

Poet, Writer
1928—

For five years, as a little girl, she could not speak. But she later gave voice to beautiful poetry. Named Marguerite Johnson at birth, she is known today by the name she later chose: Maya Angelou.

Angelou's parents divorced when she was three, and she was sent to live with her grandmother in Stamps, a small, poor, segregated town in Arkansas. She and her brother Bailey lived there for almost five years. Then Angelou left for a visit with her mother, and her life was changed forever. Her mother's boyfriend raped her. She was sent back to her grandmother's, but the terrible experience left her unable to speak. During this time, she began to read extensively.

After graduating from the eighth grade, Angelou and her brother were sent to San Francisco to live with their mother. During a summer visit with her father, there was a quarrel, and Angelou ran away. For a month she lived with other homeless teens in an old van. After returning to her mother's home, she got a job as the first African-American streetcar conductor in San Francisco. At age sixteen, Angelou gave birth to a son. She worked at a series of jobs to support him. Life was difficult.

At age twenty-two, Angelou married, but was divorced two years later.

Soon afterward, she moved to New York and became a professional dancer. In 1954, she won a part in the musical *Porgy and Bess* and toured Africa and Europe. After returning to the United States, she and Godfrey Cambridge wrote a show called *Cabaret for Freedom* in an effort to raise money for the Civil Rights Movement. Angelou continued writing stories and poetry, then moved to Africa, where she lived in Egypt and Ghana. Upon her return in 1966, she wrote the first of five autobiographical books. Titled *I Know Why the Caged Bird Sings*, it became a best-seller.

In 1971, Angelou published her first book of poetry, *Just Give Me a Cool Drink of Water 'fore I Diiie*. It was nominated for a Pulitzer Prize, and soon everybody was talking about Maya Angelou. Also in 1971, Angelou became the first African-American woman to have a screenplay made into a movie. She won acclaim as an actress and began teaching at Wake Forest University in Winston-Salem, North Carolina. In 1993, she was asked to read her work *On the Pulse of Morning* at President Bill Clinton's inauguration.

Guion Stewart Bluford, Jr.
1942—
Mae C. Jemison
1956—

Astronauts

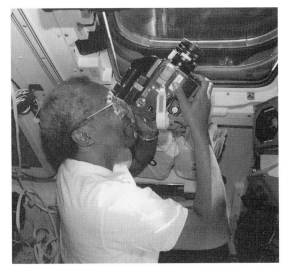

Guion Stewart Bluford, Jr.

If you want to succeed, [you must] . . . work hard, dedicate yourself and make the necessary sacrifices. . . . Once you set goals for yourself, you should doggedly pursue them until you achieve them.

—Guion Bluford

Colonel Guion Stewart Bluford, Jr., sat strapped to his seat aboard the 100-ton space shuttle *Challenger* on August 30, 1983. A few minutes after 2:30 A.M., the *Challenger* blasted off, carrying the first African-American astronaut into space.

Bluford was born in Philadelphia in 1942. He joined the Air Force in 1964 and flew 144 combat missions in Vietnam. He logged more than 3,000 hours of flying time and was awarded more than two dozen medals and awards. But Bluford wanted to do more than fly airplanes. He wanted to design them as well.

Soon after returning from Vietnam, Bluford was accepted at the U.S. Air Force Institute of Technology, where he earned a master's degree in aerospace engineering. Then he began testing new airplanes and evaluating new aircraft systems.

In 1978, Bluford received his Ph.D. in aerospace engineering with a minor in laser physics. In the same year, he applied for admittance to the astronaut program with the National Aeronautics and Space Administration (NASA). Although 8,878 people had applied, there were only 35 openings. Bluford was selected to fill one of them.

Training took place at the Johnson Space Flight Center in Houston, Texas. For six months, Bluford attended classes in aerodynamics, medicine, astronomy, geology, and communications. He spent weeks learning to operate the space shuttle's remote manipulator and working with computers, power systems, and instruments that controlled the shuttle's movements.

The U.S. space program had gotten under way in 1957, when the Soviet Union launched *Sputnik I,* a 184-pound (83.5-kg) space satellite. The American public was shocked at the Russian "first," and within a year, NASA was created. In 1961, the Soviet Union scored another first when Yuri Gagarin became the first man to orbit the earth. Twenty-three days later, the United States launched its first man in space—Commander Alan B. Shepard. By the time Bluford entered the astronaut program, the United States had taken the lead in space exploration.

In August 1983, Bluford joined the crew aboard the *Challenger,* the second U.S. space shuttle, and began a six-day flight in space, 180 miles (290 km) above the earth. During the flight, Bluford launched a $45-million Insat 1B communications and weather satellite for India. He also participated in medical tests to discover why some astronauts experience motion sickness.

On October 30, 1985, Bluford blasted off for his second *Challenger* mission. This mission consisted of 111 orbits of the earth, during which 76 scientific experiments were performed. In April 1991, Bluford took his third trip into space aboard the shuttle orbiter *Discovery* for a 199-hour, 134-orbit flight.

Mae C. Jemison

Unlike Bluford, Mae C. Jemison did not begin her career with the Air Force. Born in Decatur, Alabama, she grew up in Chicago, Illionois. She graduated from Stanford University in California with a degree in chemical engineering, then went on to attend medical school at Cornell University in New York. During this time, she worked in a refugee camp in Thailand. Jemison's continued interest in working in foreign countries led to her learning to speak Swahili, Japanese, and Russian.

After graduating from medical school, Jemison joined the Peace Corps and served as a medical officer in Sierra Leone and Liberia. She developed a self-help program for local people and supervised the health care system for both Peace Corps volunteers and U.S. Embassy personnel. After leaving the Peace Corps, Jemison decided she wanted more adventure. She applied to NASA to begin astronaut training in 1987. A year later, she served as a mission specialist on STS–47, Spacelab–J. In 1992, she won a place on the space shuttle *Endeavor*. With this mission, Jemison became the first African-American woman in space.

In 1993, Jemison left NASA and became a professor at Dartmouth College. She is now director of the Jemison Institute, which helps people in developing countries through technological change. Like Bluford, Jemison has made her mark both in space and on earth.

Muhammad Ali

Heavyweight Boxing Champion
1942—

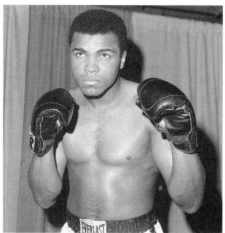

I am the greatest.

—Muhammad Ali

"Float like a butterfly, sting like a bee; his hands can't hit what his eyes can't see." This is how Muhammad Ali described his fighting style—but he did more than just bug his opponents.

Ali was born Cassius Marcellus Clay, Jr., in Louisville, Kentucky. He began boxing when he was twelve years old. He won the national Golden Glove title twice and a gold medal in the 1960 Summer Olympics in Rome, Italy. Louisville was still segregated at that time, and after being refused service in a Louisville restaurant because he was African-American, he angrily threw his Olympic medal into the Ohio River. He turned professional in October, 1960, and four years later, he defeated Sonny Liston to become heavyweight champion of the world. He then announced that he had become a member of a black religious group called the Nation of Islam and would, from then on, be known as Muhammad Ali.

Ali's announcement was met with widespread criticism. Many people regarded the leaders of the Nation of Islam as anti-white and anti-Jewish. The criticism increased when Ali asked to be excused from the military draft on the grounds that he was a Muslim minister. At that time, the United States was becoming deeply involved in the Vietnam War (early 1960s–1975).

Increasing numbers of U.S. soldiers were being sent to Vietnam to fight.

After failing a pre-induction mental test, Ali had been rejected for U.S. Army service. But in 1966, he was suddenly reclassified and drafted. He protested bitterly and refused to be inducted into the Army, saying, "No Vietcong ever called me Nigger." (The term "Vietcong," short for Vietnamese-communist, referred to the people fighting against the United States and the South Vietnamese government.) As a result, the U.S. government sentenced Ali to five years in prison. The World Boxing Association stripped him of his boxing title, and his license to fight in New York was revoked.

Ali remained free on bail while his case was being appealed, and in 1970, Judge Walter Mansfield ruled that the athletic commission had acted illegally when it took away his license to box. In 1971, the U.S. Supreme Court overturned his conviction. Later that year, in what was billed the "Fight of the Century," Ali lost to Joe Frazier. He won a rematch in 1974, although many disputed the judges' decision. Ali then regained his heavyweight title when he fought George Foreman in Africa in what was dubbed "The Rumble in the Jungle." In 1975, Ali met Frazier in the ring again. This time, the bout took place in the Philippines and was called the "Thrilla in Manila." Ali won when Frazier's manager stopped the fight. Ali lost his title to Leon Spinks in 1978 but regained it seven months later.

In 1979, Ali retired. His record stood at 56 wins, 3 losses. He successfully defended his title 19 times and was the first man to win the heavyweight crown 3 times. Ali was famous not only for his speed, footwork, and exceptional skill, but also for his rhyming predictions of victory.

Ali was later diagnosed with Parkinson's Disease, a neurological disease caused partly by the repeated blows to the head he suffered when he was boxing. In 1996, thousands of people applauded as Ali lit the flame opening the Olympic Games in Atlanta, Georgia. Many regard him as the greatest boxer of all time.

Toni Morrison

Novelist, Editor

1931—

Beloved

you are my sister

you are my daughter

You are my face; you are me

—From *Beloved*

"She paints pictures with words, and reading or hearing those words is like listening to music." This comment by Leontyne Price refers to Toni Morrison, one of the best writers of the twentieth century.

Born in Lorain, Ohio, Morrison was christened Chloe Anthony Wofford. Her mother's family were sharecroppers from Greenville, Alabama, who moved north after losing their land. Her father's family came from Georgia.

Morrison's early life was filled with tales of other worlds and other times. Some she heard from her grandmother, who conscientiously kept a record of her dreams in a small notebook. Others she heard from her parents, who were wonderful storytellers. Like roots of a tree, memories of these childhood songs, stories, and folklore were to nourish and support the creations of her own imagination.

When Morrison started school, she was the only African-American child in her first-grade class and the only one who could read. Her love of reading continued into adolescence as she immersed herself in the great American and Russian novels. Encouraged by her family, Morrison finished high school and went on to receive a bachelor of arts from Howard University in 1953. Two years later, she received her master's degree from Cornell University and returned to Howard to teach and write. While there, she met Harold Morrison, an architecture student from Jamaica, and married him.

Soon after her second son was born, Morrison began working as a textbook editor in the Syracuse, New York, offices of Random House. Later, she became senior editor and worked at the company's New York City office. Her position allowed her to help and encourage many young black writers and to arrange for the publication of books on African-American history.

It was Morrison's own writing that established her as a major figure in American literature. Her first four novels—*The Bluest Eye, Sula, Song of Solomon* (which won the National Book Critics Circle Award), and *Tar Baby*—reflect both the pain and the beauty of the African-American experience. Her fifth novel, *Beloved,* won the Pulitzer Prize for Literature in 1988. Based on the true story of a slave named Margaret Garner, who killed her own baby daughter rather than see her live as a slave, *Beloved* is an intensely felt ghost story laced with sorrow, poetry, and pain.

Morrison's genius as a writer lies in her ability to draw readers into the world she creates. The emotions she calls forth tie us to her characters, forcing us to feel their loneliness and love.

In 1993, Morrison became the first African-American woman to win the Nobel Prize in literature. She currently holds a position as Goheen Professor in the Humanities at Princeton University.

Jesse Jackson

Minister, Civil Rights Leader

1941—

America is like a quilt—many patches, many pieces, many colors, many sizes, all woven and held together by a common thread. . . . all of us count and fit somewhere.

—Jesse Jackson

Born in Greenville, South Carolina, Jesse Jackson graduated from Sterling High School and received a football scholarship to the University of Illinois. Not long after enrolling there, he transferred to North Carolina Agricultural and Technical College at Greensboro and became active in the sit-in movement.

After graduating, Jackson entered Chicago Theological Seminary and continued his involvement in the Civil Rights Movement. In 1965, he met Martin Luther King, Jr., at the famous Selma March and became a member of the SCLC staff. Returning to Chicago, he began preparing for King's "Campaign to End Slums." Jackson was made head of the Chicago branch of Operation Breadbasket, an organization established by King in 1962. One of its purposes was to expand job opportunities for African-Americans.

Under Jackson's direction, businesses that discriminated against blacks were boycotted, a tactic that proved very effective. Within a short time, many companies agreed to hire African-American employees, contract with

African-American–owned service companies, and utilize African-American–owned banks.

Resigning from SCLC and Operation Breadbasket in 1971, Jackson founded Operation PUSH (People United to Serve Humanity), which aimed at improving the economic status of African-Americans. Again threatening to boycott businesses, Jackson persuaded many national companies, such as Burger King, to set up African-American distributorships and spend millions of dollars advertising in black newspapers and magazines. In 1976, Jackson began PUSH for Excellence, a program designed to help African-American students get a better education.

Realizing that economic growth depended on political power, Jackson began touring the country to encourage voter registration. He preached the same message everywhere: use the power of the ballot box to elect officials who will be sympathetic to the needs of the poor, African-Americans in particular.

Eventually, Jackson became interested in international affairs. In 1979, with the hope of establishing dialogue among the Jews, Arabs, Palestinians, and other hostile groups in the Middle East, Jackson traveled to Israel, Lebanon, Egypt, and Syria. He met with Egyptian president Anwar Sadat, Syrian president Hafez al-Assad, and Palestinian leader Yasser Arafat. In terms of bringing about Arab-Israeli peace, he accomplished little. But in 1984, Jackson was able to draw on his friendship with Assad to obtain the release of U.S. Navy pilot Robert Goodman, who was taken prisoner after his plane was shot down during U.S. military operations in Lebanon. The same year, Jackson visited Cuba and obtained the release of twenty-two Americans and twenty-six Cubans in prison there.

The year 1984 was significant for Jesse Jackson for another reason. It was the year he first sought the Democratic nomination for president of the United States. An African-American presidential campaign was needed, he said, to demonstrate to politicians, both Democrats and Republicans, that the concerns of African-Americans could not be ignored.

Although he was the clear favorite among African-Americans, Jackson also needed white votes to win the nomination. He put together what he called the Rainbow Coalition and began addressing the concerns of women, Hispanics, the poor, the handicapped, the young, and anyone else who felt they were being ignored by the other candidates. By the time of the Democratic convention in San Francisco, Jackson had the support of more than 450 delegates. It wasn't enough to win, but it was impressive.

In 1988, Jackson again sought the Democratic nomination. Previously, many political leaders had scoffed at the idea of a successful African-American presidential candidate. The country was not ready, they said. But Jackson showed them up. He enlarged his base of African-American support while gathering thousands of white votes. Although he didn't win, he came close. In doing so, Jackson forced the country to take the idea of an African-American president seriously and insured the continuance of African-American political power.

After the election, Jackson worked as a special presidential envoy in Africa. In April 1999, he negotiated the release of three U.S. soldiers being held captive by Yugoslav president Slobodan Milosevic.

John Robert Lewis

Civil Rights Leader, U.S. Congressman
1940 —

John Robert Lewis grew up to give speeches before Congress. As a child, he developed his speaking skills by preaching to the chickens on his parents' farm. The only problem was that the chickens were intended for the dinner table, and after preaching to them, Lewis could never find it in his heart to eat them.

Lewis was born in Pike County, Alabama, the third of ten children. His parents were poor, and his home had no electricity or running water. The community was segregated, and opportunities for African-Americans were limited. In 1955, a fourteen-year-old African-American boy named Emmett Till was lynched in Mississippi, and Lewis began to think about what he could do to end racial injustice. That same year, Rosa Parks refused to move to the back of a bus in Montgomery, Alabama. Her action set off the famous Montgomery bus boycott. These two events had a tremendous impact on Lewis.

In 1957, Lewis entered the American Baptist Theological Seminary in Nashville, Tennessee, where he learned about the nonviolent philosophies of Mahatma Gandhi, who led India to independence, and American writer Henry Thoreau, who protested the Mexican War (1846–48). Their beliefs were to influence Lewis when he became involved in the Civil Rights Movement.

Lewis began by taking part in sit-ins and boycotts in Nashville. Becoming increasingly involved in the movement, he helped found a new civil rights group called the Student Nonviolent Coordinating Committee (SNCC). In 1961, Lewis joined the Freedom Riders, who were protesting segregation on buses traveling across the country. They were attacked by segregationists in Anniston, Alabama.

Lewis refused to quit. Over the next few years, he suffered numerous beatings and was arrested forty times for civil rights activities. In 1963, Lewis was elected chairman of SNCC. One week after his election, Lewis and five other African-American leaders met with President John F. Kennedy to discuss a proposed civil rights bill and the upcoming March on Washington. The march was a huge success, and Lewis gave a fiery speech there.

As attacks on civil rights workers became increasingly brutal, many civil rights activists began to doubt whether nonviolent tactics could succeed in ending racial injustice. This was especially true among the students working for SNCC. In 1966, Lewis was replaced as SNCC chairman by Stokely Carmichael, as many SNCC members turned against peaceful tactics and were no longer willing to associate with whites. But Lewis remained strongly committed to the principles of Gandhi and Martin Luther King, Jr., and he refused to turn against white people with whom he had worked for years. He resigned from SNCC on July 22, 1966.

When John F. Kennedy's brother Robert decided to run for president in 1968, Lewis joined his campaign. Ten years later, Lewis became associate director of ACTION, the federal agency that oversees the Peace Corps. In 1982, he was elected to the Atlanta City Council. In 1986, he was elected to Congress, where he remains today. Lewis continues to support antipoverty programs and efforts to extend and protect civil liberties. His autobiography is titled *Walking With the Wind*.

Bill Cosby

Comedian, Author, Philanthropist
1937—

I wasn't always black . . . there was this freckle,
and it got bigger and bigger.

—Bill Cosby

Bill Cosby has spent his life making people laugh. Born in Pennsylvania, his stories about his childhood friends Fat Albert and Weird Harold became the basis for a cartoon series, *Fat Albert and the Cosby Kids*. Life was not always so promising, however.

As a teenager, Cosby dropped out of high school to join the Navy. Education was important to him, and while in the Navy he managed to get his high school diploma. After he was discharged, he enrolled at Temple University and began his career as a comedian. He was so funny that he was offered a chance to perform on *The Tonight Show* on NBC in 1963. Two years later, he became the first African-American man to land a regular leading role on a dramatic series when he teamed with Robert Culp in the hit show *I Spy*, for which Cosby won an Emmy Award.

Movie roles soon followed, along with Grammy Award-winning comedy records, television shows, and appearances before standing-room-only crowds. Then, in 1984, Cosby made television history with *The Cosby Show*, in which he starred as Heathcliff Huxtable, a happily married father of five children. For three straight years, the show remained at the top of the Nielsen television ratings. More than 38 million people watched the show every week, and many looked up to Cosby as the perfect husband and father. *The Cosby Show* continued until 1992.

During his hit show's run, Cosby also became an author, with books such as *Fatherhood*, which stayed on the *New York Times* Best Seller List for 54 weeks, and *Time Flies*. He was also a sought-after spokesman for various commercial products. One of the richest men in the United States, Cosby was noted for his generosity and support for education and civil rights. In 1989, he and his wife Camille donated $20 million to Spelman College in Atlanta, Georgia.

In 1997, tragedy struck the Cosby family when Cosby's only son, Ennis, was killed in a robbery. The murder shocked people around the world. Thousands of people who adored Cosby mourned with him and wrote to offer sympathy.

Cosby continues to work in television and has created several other series. However, none of these shows has had the impact of *The Cosby Show*, which Coretta Scott King described as "the most positive portrayal of black family life that has ever been broadcast."

Colin Luther Powell

Secretary of State, General
1937–

There is nothing that a black boy or girl can't be—not if they put their mind to it.

—Colin Powell

Colin Luther Powell was born in New York City after his parents emigrated to the United States from Jamaica. After graduating from the City College of New York with a degree in geology, he received a commission as a second lieutenant in the U.S. Army. Powell's duties took him all over the country, from Fort Denvens, Massachusetts, to Fort Leavenworth, Kansas, to Fort Carson, Colorado. In 1962, he was sent to Vietnam. He returned home after being wounded, but later went back for a second tour of duty from 1968 to 1969. Although injured in a helicopter crash, he helped rescue other people from the burning aircraft.

In 1972, Powell received an appointment as a White House Fellow in the Nixon administration. A few years later, in 1976, he became commander of the 2nd Brigade, 101st Airborne Division, at Fort Campbell, Kentucky. In 1983, Powell became military assistant to Defense Secretary Caspar Weinberger. He was involved in the U.S. invasion of Grenada in the Caribbean, and later helped plan air raids against Libya in retaliation for terrorist activities.

In 1987, Powell became national security advisor to President Ronald Reagan. Two years later, in 1989, President George Bush promoted Powell over more senior generals to become the first African-American chairman of the Joint Chiefs of Staff. There he supervised the U.S. invasion of Panama in 1989 and the Persian Gulf War in 1991. Powell's winning strategy was based on his belief that when military action is indicated, the military should attack with overwhelming force right from the beginning, rather than go in with a smaller number of troops and then increase them, as was the case in Vietnam.

Powell retired from active duty in 1993 after being awarded numerous military awards and decorations, including the Defense Distinguished Service Medal, Defense Superior Service Medal, the Legion of Merit, the Bronze Star, and the Purple Heart. He was also honored by the governments of Argentina, Brazil, France, Jamaica, Japan, Korea, Kuwait, Saudi Arabia, Greece, and Canada. Queen Elizabeth II of England granted him an honorary knighthood. He also received the Presidential Medal of Freedom.

After retiring, Powell headed America's Promise, an organization dedicated to helping young people. In 1995, he published his autobiography, *My American Journey*, in 1995. Powell now serves on the boards of several nonprofit organizations, including Howard University and the United Negro College Fund. In December 2000, newly elected President George W. Bush made Powell the first African-American U.S. secretary of state.

Alice Walker

Writer
1944 —

Alice Walker was the eighth child of Willie Lee and Minnie Walker. Her parents were sharecroppers in Eatonton, Georgia. She began first grade early at the age of four, partly because her mother had to go to work and could not watch her. At age eight, Walker began writing poetry. In that year, Walker's brother shot her in the eye with a BB gun. She lost her sight in that eye, and felt the scar ruined her looks. Her self-confidence suffered, and her grades began to drop. Then, when she was fourteen, the scar tissue was removed, and suddenly Walker felt wonderful. Her grades improved, and when she graduated from high school she was chosen valedictorian and voted "Most Popular."

Because Walker was half-blind she was eligible for a scholarship, and the African-American community in Eatonton raised $75 to help her get to Atlanta so that she could attend Spelman College. After two years, she transferred to Sarah Lawrence College, where she graduated in 1965. She then moved to Mississippi to work with the Civil Rights Movement in its drive to register African-American voters. She also worked with the Head Start program and taught at Jackson State College and Tougaloo College.

In 1968, Walker's first book of poetry, *Once,* was published. In 1967, she married a civil-rights worker named Melvyn Leventhal. They soon had a daughter named Rebecca, born just three days after Walker finished writing her first novel, *The Third Life of Grange Copeland*.

In 1971, Walker traveled to Boston to teach a course about African-American women writers at Wellesley College and the University of Massachusetts. One of the women she discussed was Zora Neale Hurston, whose book *Their Eyes Were Watching God* was one of Walker's favorites. In 1973, Walker published her second book of poetry, *Revolutionary Petunias & Other Poems*. This was followed by her second novel, *Meridian*.

Walker and Leventhal divorced in 1977, and Walker began work on what would become her most successful book, *The Color Purple*. Published in 1982, it won the Pulitzer Prize and the National Book Award and was made into a hit movie (1985) featuring Oprah Winfrey. Walker has continued to write both poetry and novels. Her later books include *The Temple of My Familiar*, *By the Light of My Father's Smile*, and *Possessing the Secret of Joy*, a novel about learning to triumph over evil. For many students, the secret of joy is having one of Walker's books to read.

Arthur Robert Ashe, Jr.

Tennis Player
1943–1993

Arthur Ashe grew up to become a world-famous tennis champion. As a child, however, he was prevented from playing on most public courts or competing in many tournaments because he was African-American. Born in Richmond, Virginia, Ashe learned to play tennis at Brookfield Park. His playing was so impressive that he caught the attention of R. Walter Johnson, who had coached tennis great Althea Gibson, the first African-American to play professional tennis. As a thirteen-year-old, Ashe himself shattered a racial barrier when he became the first African-American to compete in the boys' tennis championships in Maryland.

In 1961, Ashe entered UCLA on a tennis scholarship. Two years later, he became the first African-American man to join the U.S. Davis Cup team. Over the next fifteen years he set a winning record that would stand until 1984. In 1965, Ashe, representing UCLA, won the NCAA men's singles championship. Remembering the difficulty he had had as a tennis player in a segregated world, Ashe helped establish the National Junior Tennis League in 1968 to help poor children develop their tennis skills. That same year he also became the first African-American man to win the U.S. Open.

Ashe's concern for human rights led him to protest apartheid (an extensive system of segregation) in South Africa. Because of his actions, the South African government refused Ashe's request for a visa to enter the country in 1970. Three years later, however, the South African government reversed its decision, and Ashe became the first black man to play in South Africa's national championships. Then, in 1975, Ashe became the first African-American to win the men's singles title at Wimbledon when he defeated Jimmy Connors.

Following a heart attack in 1979, Ashe underwent quadruple-bypass surgery. The following year he retired as a professional tennis player with a record of 818 wins, including 51 titles. Ashe did not give up his interest in the sport, however. He became captain of the U.S. Davis Cup team in 1980. Three years later, he was forced to undergo more surgery, during which he received a blood transfusion. Unfortunately, the blood was contaminated with the HIV virus that causes AIDS. At the time, however, no one knew this. Ashe continued his effort to end apartheid in South Africa. He was also active in the drive to raise academic standards for college athletes. Over the years, Ashe wrote several books: *A Hard Road to Glory: A History of the African-American Athlete, Off the Court,* and *Days of Grace.*

Ashe died of AIDS in 1993. A statue of him, holding books and a tennis racket, stands on Monument Avenue in Richmond.

Henry Louis "Hank" Aaron

Baseball Player

1934 —

As a professional baseball player, Hank Aaron was often cheered as he rounded home plate. But those cheers never sounded better than when he hit his 715th home run and broke the lifetime home run record set by Babe Ruth many years earlier.

The third of eight children, Aaron grew up in Mobile, Alabama. His high school did not have a baseball team, but Aaron joined a semi-pro team called the Mobile Black Bears during his junior year. Until 1947, when Jackie Robinson joined the Brooklyn Dodgers, professional baseball was segregated, and African-Americans played in a separate Negro League. Over the next few years, white teams began hiring African-American players, but Aaron began his career in 1951 with the all-black Indiana Clowns. They paid him $200 a month.

Aaron had had no real training. He batted cross-handed, with his left hand above his right, until a Milwaukee Braves (now Atlanta Braves) scout named Dewey Griggs had him change his style—right in the middle of a game. Nevertheless, Aaron led the Negro League with a .467 average.

The Braves purchased Aaron's contract for $10,000 and, after playing with the Braves farm club, he joined the Braves organization in 1954. Three years later, he was named National League MVP. Over the years Aaron hit home run after home run. As he came closer to breaking Ruth's record, Aaron began receiving hate mail and threats from racists who did not want an African-American to take the number one spot. Aaron just kept on hitting.

On April 8, 1974, Hank Aaron did it! Home run number 715 was scored in a game against the Los Angeles Dodgers; the ball traveled 385 feet (117 meters). Aaron continued playing until 1976, when he retired with a home run total of 755. He became a vice-president with the Atlanta Braves organization. In 1982, Aaron was elected to the Baseball Hall of Fame.

Oprah Winfrey

Television Talk Show Host, Actress, Movie Producer

1954—

How can I use this life? How can I be of value, real value?

—Oprah Winfrey

She owns and produces her own television show, has produced and starred in award-winning movies, has her own magazine, and is one of the richest women in the world. But first Oprah Winfrey had to overcome early years of poverty and pain. Winfrey was born in Kosciusko, Mississippi, where she lived with her grandmother until age three, when she moved in with her mother in Milwaukee. Her life in Milwaukee was miserable. She was an abused child and ran away as a teenager. She developed behavior problems and at thirteen was sent to Nashville, Tennessee, to live with her father. This was a better atmosphere, and Winfrey thrived.

While still in high school, Winfrey got a job with WVOL radio. In 1971, she became Nashville's first female African-American news anchor when she was hired by WTVF–TV. After graduating from Tennessee State University, Winfrey moved to Baltimore, Maryland, where she began working as a news anchor for WJZ–TV. Two years later, she became co-host of *Baltimore Is Talking*. In 1984, she moved to Chicago to host *AM Chicago* on WLS–TV. The show had not been doing well, but after Winfrey began hosting it, it became so popular that it was renamed the *Oprah Winfrey Show*. It soon became the most popular talk show in the country.

In 1985, Winfrey was nominated for an Oscar for her performance in *The Color Purple*, a movie based on a book by African-American writer Alice Walker. She also appeared in a film version of *Native Son*, based on the work of Richard Wright, another African-American author. In 1988, Winfrey established her own company, Harpo Productions ("Harpo" is "Oprah" spelled backwards) and began producing movies and television specials. Among them were *The Women of Brewster Place, Kaffir Boy*, and *Beloved*, a movie based on the Pulitzer Prize-winning novel by Toni Morrison. In 1989, Winfrey donated $1 million to Morehouse College, a historically African-American college in Atlanta, Georgia.

During her lonely, unhappy childhood, Winfrey spent many hours reading, and in 1996, she decided to encourage others to read by creating a book club on her show. Her plan worked. Every book she discussed on her show became a best-seller. Today, *The Oprah Winfrey Show* is watched by millions of viewers in over one hundred countries and has won numerous awards, including several Emmys. In April 2000, Winfrey began publication of a magazine whose title is simply *O*. She is said to be worth more than half a billion dollars, but her tremendous influence is priceless.

Michael Jeffrey Jordan

Basketball Player
1963—

*The basketball court for me, during a game,
is the most peaceful place I can imagine.*

—Michael Jordan

Experts agree that Michael Jordan is the best basketball player in the history of the sport. Most people, then, would never guess that he was cut from his high school team when he was fifteen. This incident taught Jordan to deal with disappointment and made him determined to improve his game. And improve he did! As a freshman at the University of North Carolina in 1982, Jordan made the game-winning shot with 17 seconds left to play to give North Carolina the NCAA title. Later, when he played for the Chicago Bulls, he always wore a pair of University of North Carolina shorts under his Bulls uniform for luck. He also kept his North Carolina number—23.

In 1984, the 6-foot, 6-inch (2-m) Jordan was a member of the winning U.S. basketball team at the Seoul Olympics. A year later, in 1985, as a member of the Chicago Bulls, he was named Rookie of the Year. Famous for his slam-dunk, Jordan's incredible jumping ability earned him the nickname

"Air" Jordan. He led the Bulls to three consecutive national championships and was top NBA scorer from 1987 to 1991. Then, in 1992, he won a second gold medal as a member of the U.S. Olympic "Dream Team" in Barcelona, Spain.

In 1993, Jordan's father was murdered during a carjacking. It was a terrible blow. Jordan had always been close to his parents, who had attended many of his games. Two months later, Jordan retired from basketball, saying he needed another challenge. He did not give up sports, however. Instead, he joined the Birmingham Barons, a Chicago White Sox farm club, in an effort to become a professional baseball player. But he later reconsidered and returned to the Bulls in 1995. He retired again in 1999 after achieving 29,277 career points and a career scoring average of 31.5. By this time Jordan had led his team to six national championships, won ten NBA scoring titles, and been named Most Valuable Player five times. He had also become an enormously popular spokesman for various commercial products, and even starred in the movie *Space Jam* (1996).

After retiring, Jordan became president of basketball operations for the Washington Wizards. When asked in a fall 1993 *Newsweek* interview if he had any regrets, Jordan said no, explaining, "You're only bitter if you reach the end of your life and you're filled with frustration because . . . you regret not accomplishing the things you could have accomplished."

Benjamin S. Carson

Pediatric Neurosurgeon

1951—

Benjamin S. Carson was born in Detroit, Michigan, the younger of two brothers. His parents divorced when he was young, and Carson soon developed a terrible temper. He had difficulty in school, and his classmates called him "dummy." His poor grades upset his mother, who limited the amount of television he could watch and told him he would have to read two books a week.

His mother's plan worked. Within a year, Carson had become first in his class. He still had a short temper, however. When Carson was fourteen, he tried to stab another student. The knife broke when it struck the other child's belt buckle, and Carson was so shocked at what he had done that he ran home, locked himself in the bathroom, and prayed to God for help. His prayers were answered. Carson later said he never lost his temper again, and he remains extremely religious. He continued to read widely and decided to become a physician.

In 1973, Carson graduated from Yale University with a degree in psychology. He then entered medical school at the University of Michigan, where he became a surgeon specializing in operations involving the brain and the nervous system. After he graduated in 1977, he went to work at

Johns Hopkins Hospital in Baltimore, Maryland. There he became director of pediatric neurosurgery in 1985. In 1987, Carson made medical history when he successfully separated a pair of twins who were joined to each other at the back of the head. Others had attempted to separate twins joined in this way, but those operations had always resulted in the death of one or both children. Carson also successfully removed half the brain of several children suffering from multiple seizures.

Today, Carson performs as many as five hundred operations a year. He and his wife, Candy, have established the Carson Scholars Fund to provide college scholarships for poor children. He has written three books: *Gifted Hands, Think Big,* and *The Big Picture.*

Shelton Jackson "Spike" Lee

Movie Director, Producer
1957–

I've been blessed with the opportunity to express the views of black people who otherwise don't have access to power and the media.

—Spike Lee

Shelton Jackson "Spike" Lee grew up in a show business family. His father, Bill Lee, was a jazz musician who would later compose the music for Lee's movies. Born in Atlanta, Georgia, Lee grew up in Brooklyn, New York, where most of his films would be set.

After graduating from Morehouse College, Lee entered New York University's Institute of Film and Television. In 1982, he won the Student Academy Award for *Joe's Bed-Stuy Barbershop: We Cut Heads*. "Bed-Stuy" referred to Bedford-Stuyvesant, a neighborhood in New York City. In 1986, Lee became known across the country for his hit movie, *She's Gotta Have It*. He spent $125,000 to make the film, which earned $8 million and won the Los Angeles Film Critics New Generation award, as well as the Prix de Jeuness at the Cannes Film Festival in France. Suddenly, all the big movie studios were interested in Spike Lee. His next movie was *School Daze*, a movie about college students. Lee followed that with *Do the Right Thing*

(1989), which was nominated for an Oscar for best screenplay.

Lee's movies often focus on historic events and people. *Malcolm X* (1992) honors the Black Power leader. *Get on the Bus* concerns the Million Man March that took place in Washington, D.C., in 1995 to promote unity among African-American men. *Four Little Girls* (1997) tells the story of the four children who died in the 1963 bombing of the Sixteenth Street Baptist Church in Birmingham, Alabama, when segregationists tried to stop the Civil Rights Movement.

Although Lee is the most successful African-American film director today, movies were not his first love. When he was growing up, Lee wanted to be a professional baseball player. In fact, he named his son Satchel, for legendary baseball pitcher Satchel Paige. He is also a big New York Knicks fan and often goes to their games. In 1998, Lee directed a basketball movie called *He Got Game*.

In addition to focusing on African-American people and issues, Lee regularly employs African-Americans when making his movies. Many black actors got their first starring roles in his movies. The African-American community has long been concerned that white movie makers, no matter how well intentioned, could not accurately depict the African-American experience. They believe the movie industry would greatly benefit from the influence of African-American writers, directors, producers, and other behind-the-scenes people. Because of Lee, people from all over the world have seen movies from an African-American point of view.

Tiger Woods
Golfer
1975–

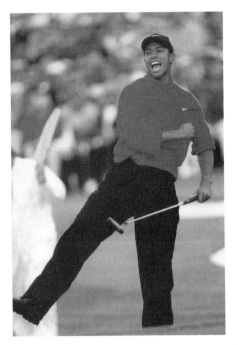

Tiger Woods started playing golf when he was barely old enough to hold a golf club. He was born in Cypress, California, in 1975, the same year that Lee Elder became the first African-American to play in the Masters Tournament in Augusta, Georgia. At age two, Woods appeared on television in a putting exhibition with comedian Bob Hope. Woods attended Stanford University for two years, then turned professional in 1996 after winning three consecutive U.S. Amateur Championships. He changed his given name, Eldrick, to Tiger, the nickname his father, Earl, had given him in honor of a South Vietnamese army officer with whom Earl had served in Vietnam.

In 1997, Woods was named Professional Golfers' Association (PGA) Rookie of the Year after winning the Masters Tournament by a twelve-point margin. Proud of his racial heritage, Woods began to describe himself as "Cablinasian"—a word he invented to mean part black, part white, part Native American, and part Asian. This angered some black leaders who wanted him to emphasize only his African-American heritage, but Woods was determined to embrace his entire background.

In 1999, Woods won the 81st PGA Championship, beating Sergio Garcia by one point. It was his fourteenth worldwide tournament victory. The next year he made golf history again when he won the U.S. Open at Pebble Beach by fifteen strokes—the biggest margin of victory in the history of any major tournament. Then, in July 2000, Woods won the British Open by a record-breaking nineteen under par to become the youngest player ever to accomplish a career Grand Slam. (For a career Grand Slam, a player must win the Masters, the PGA Championship, the U.S. Open, and the British Open.)

Golf has traditionally been a predominantly white sport. Until recently, African-Americans were refused admittance to most golf courses. In addition to earning him millions of dollars in prize money and endorsements, Woods's exciting play has made him a favorite with golf fans worldwide and encouraged millions of African-American and other minority teenagers to try the sport.

Elizabeth Eckford's Account of Day One at Central High School

You remember the day before we were to go in, we met Superintendent Blossom at the school board office. He told us what the mob might say and do but he never told us we wouldn't have any protection. He told our parents not to come because he wouldn't be able to protect the children if they did.

That night I was so excited I couldn't sleep. The next morning I was about the first one up. While I was pressing my black and white dress—I had made it to wear on the first day of school—my little brother turned on the TV set. They started telling about a large crowd gathered at the school. . . .

Before I left home Mother called us into the living-room. She said we should have a word of prayer. Then I caught the bus and got off a block from the school. I saw a large crowd of people standing across the street from the soldiers guarding Central. As I walked on, the crowd got suddenly very quiet. Superintendent Blossom had told us to enter by the front door. I looked at all the people and thought, "Maybe I will be safer if I walk down the block to the front entrance behind the guards."

At the corner I tried to pass through the long line of guards around the school so as to enter the grounds behind them. One of the guards pointed across the street. So I pointed in the same direction and asked whether he meant for me to cross the street and walk down. He nodded "yes." So I walked across the street, conscious of the crowd that stood there, but they moved away from me.

For a moment all I could hear was the shuffling of their feet. Then someone shouted, "Here she comes, get ready!" I moved away from the crowd on the sidewalk and into the street. If the mob came at me I could then cross back over so the guards could protect me.

The crowd moved in closer and then began to follow me, calling me names. I still wasn't afraid. Just a little bit nervous. Then my knees started to shake all of a sudden and I wondered whether I could make it to the center entrance a block away. It was the longest block I ever walked in my whole life.

Even so, I still wasn't too scared because all the time I kept thinking that the guards would protect me.

When I got right in front of the school, I went up to a guard again. But this time he just looked straight ahead and didn't move to let me pass him. I didn't know what to do. Then I looked and saw that the path leading to the front entrance was a little further ahead. So I walked until I was right in front of the path to the front door.

I stood looking at the school—it looked so big! Just then the guards let some white students go through.

The crowd was quiet. I guess they were waiting to see what was going to happen. When I was able to steady my knees, I walked up to the guard who had let the white students in. He too didn't move. When I tried to squeeze past him, he raised his bayonet and then the other guards closed in and they raised their bayonets.

They glared at me with a mean look and I was very frightened and didn't know what to do. I turned around and the crowd came toward me.

They moved closer and closer. Somebody started yelling, "Lynch her! Lynch her!"

I tried to see a friendly face somewhere in the mob—someone who maybe would help. I looked into the face of an old woman and it seemed a kind face, but when I looked at her again, she spat on me.

They came closer, shouting, "No nigger bitch is going to get in our school. Get out of here!"

I turned back to the guards but their faces told me I wouldn't get help from them. Then I looked down the block and saw a bench at the bus stop. I thought, "If I can get there I will be safe." I don't know why the bench seemed a safe place to me, but I started walking toward it. I tried to close my mind to what they were shouting, and kept saying to myself, "If I can only make it to the bench I will be safe."

When I finally got there, I don't think I could have gone another step. I sat down and the mob crowded up and began shouting all over again. Someone hollered, "Drag her over to this tree! Let's take care of this nigger." Just then a white man sat down beside me, put his arm around me and patted my shoulder. He raised my chin and said, "Don't let them see you cry."

Then a white lady—she was very nice—she came over to me on the bench. She spoke to me but I don't remember now what she said. She put me on the bus and sat next to me. She asked me my name and tried to talk to me but I don't think I answered. I can't remember much about the bus ride, but the next thing I remember I was standing in front of the School for the Blind, where Mother works.

I thought, "Maybe she isn't here. But she has to be here!" So I ran upstairs, and I think some teachers tried to talk to me, but I kept running until I reached Mother's classroom.

Mother was standing at the window with her head bowed, but she must have sensed I was there because she turned around. She looked as if she had been crying, and I wanted to tell her I was all right. But I couldn't speak. She put her arms around me and I cried.

Organizations
and Online Sites

The African American Journey
http://www.pbs.org/aajourney/

The African American Journey
http://www.worldbook.com/fun/aajourny/
html/index.html

African-Americans in the Sciences
http://www.princeton.edu/~mcbrown/
display/faces.html

The Black Patriots Foundation
1612 K Street NW #1104
Washington, DC 20006-2802
(202) 452-1776
http://www.blackpatriots.org

**Martin Luther King, Jr.
Papers Project**
http://www.stanford.edu/group/King/

**National Association for the
Advancement of Colored People**
4805 Mt. Hope Drive
Baltimore, MD 21215
(410) 521-4939
www.naacp.org

Rainbow/PUSH Coalition
930 East 50th Street
Chicago, IL 60615-2702
(773) 373-3366
www.rainbowpush.org

**Smithsonian: African American
History and Culture Resources**
http://www.si.edu/resource/faq/nmah/
afroam.htm

The United Nations
Public Inquiries Unit
GA-57
New York, NY 10017
(212) 963-4475
E-mail: inquiries@un.org
www.un.org

For Further Reading

Altman, Susan. *The Encyclopedia of African-American Heritage,* 2nd ed. New York: Facts on File, 2000.

Foner, Philip S. and Ronald L. Lewis. *Black Workers.* Philadelphia: Temple University Press, 1989.

Hardy, P. Stephen and Sheila Jackson Hardy. *Extraordinary People of the Harlem Renaissance.* Danbury, CT: Children's Press, 2000.

Leckie, William H. *The Buffalo Soldiers: A Narrative of the Negro Cavalry in the West.* Norman: University of Oklahoma Press, 1985.

McGowen, Tom. *African-Americans in the Old West.* Danbury, CT: Children's Press, 1998.

Newman, Shirlee P. *Slavery in the United States.* Danbury, CT: Franklin Watts, 2000.

Selfridge, John. *John Coltrane.* Danbury, CT: Franklin Watts, 1999.

Stein, R. Conrad. *The Underground Railroad.* Danbury, CT: Children's Press, 1997.

Williams, Juan. *Eyes on the Prize: America's Civil Rights Years 1954–1965.* New York: Viking, 1987.

Witherspoon, William Roger. *Martin Luther King, Jr., . . . To the Mountain Top.* New York: Doubleday & Company, 1985.

Index

Numbers in *italics* represent illustrations.

Aaron, Henry Louis "Hank," *261,* 261–62
Abbott, Robert Sengstacke, *122,* 122–23, 136–37
Abele, Julian Francis, *165,* 165–66
abolitionists, 30–31, 32–33, 52, 56, 57–58, 59–60, 61–62, 63–65, 66–67, 146
Abraham (slave), 41
ACTION, 252
acting profession, 167–68, 263–64
Adams, John Quincy, 46
Addams, Jane, 113
African-American Civil War Soldiers, 71, *72,* 72–75, 78, 89
African Legion, 139
African Methodist Episcopal Church (AME), 33
African Methodist Episcopal Zion Church, 62
agriculture, 96–97
Ailey, Alvin, *227,* 227, *228,* 228
Ali, Muhammad, 236, *244,* 244–45
Allan, Lewis, 160
Allen, Richard, *32,* 32–33
All God's Chillun Got Wings, 167
Amistad, 45, 46
Anderson, Marian, *171,* 171, *172,* 172–73
Angelou, Maya, *239,* 239–40
Anthony, Susan B., 52, 113
anthropology, 119–21, 144–45
architecture, 165–66
Armistead, James, *28,* 28–29
Armstrong, Louis, 131, *142,* 142–43, 160
Armstrong, Samuel C., 80
Arnold, Benedict, 28

art, 107–8. *See also* dance; photography; writers
Ashe, Arthur Robert, Jr., *259,* 259–60
Ashley, John, 30–31
Ashley, William Henry, 48–49
Association for the Study of Negro Life and History (ASNLH), 151, 152
astronauts, 241–43
astronomy, 22–23
Attucks, Crispus, *20,* 20, *21,* 21, 58
Autobiography of Malcolm X, 202

Bailey, Frederick Augustus Washington. *See* Douglass, Frederick
Baker, Ella Josephine, *204,* 204–5
Baldwin, James, *194,* 194–96
Banjo Lesson, The, 108
Banneker, Benjamin, *22,* 22–23
Barrow, Joseph Louis. *See* Louis, Joe
"Bar's Fight, The," 16, 17
baseball, 174–75, 181–83, 261–62
Basie, Count, 160
basketball, 265–66
Baumfree, Isabella. *See* Truth, Sojourner
Beauregard, General, 70
Beckwourth, James Pierson, 48, 48–49
Beloved, 246, 247, 264
Benjamin-Constant, Jean-Joseph, 107
Bennett, Rolla, 38
Bennett, Ned, 38
Bethel African Methodist Episcopal Church, 33
Bethune, Mary McLeod, 103, 117, 117–18, 152
Binga, Jesse, 137

Birth of the Cool, 190
"Black, Brown, and Beige," 154
Black Boy, 164
Black Codes, 76
Black Cross Nurses, 139
Black Eagle Flying Corps, 139
Black History Week, 152
Black Muslims, 221–22, 235
Black nationalist, 138–30
Black Panther Party, 234–35
Black Power Movement, 185, 234–36
Black Reconstruction in America, 120
Black Seminoles, *40,* 40–42
Black Star Line, 139
Blair, Ezell, Jr., *213,* 213
blood, study of, 178–80
blues music, 126–27, 130–31
Bluest Eye, The, 247
Bluford, Guion Stewart, Jr., *241,* 241–43
Boston Massacre, 20–21
boxing, 169–70, 244–45
boycott, 113, 200–201, 212, 230, 248, 251
Braddock, James, 170
Breedlove, Sarah. *See* Walker, Madam C. J.
Brotherhood of Sleeping Car Porters, 176,
    177
Brown, John, 107
"Brown Bomber." *See* Louis, Joe
Brown v. Board of Education, 145, 207, 210
Bruce, Blanche K., 77
Buffalo Soldiers, 89–90
Bunche, Ralph, *188,* 188–89
Bunker Hill, Battle of, 26
Burns, Anthony, 58
bus desegregation, 199–201, 215–17, 230, 251
business woman, 102–3
By the Light of My Father's Smile, 258

Cabaret for Freedom, 240
Caesar, John, 41
Cain, Richard, 77

Cambridge, Godfrey, 240
Carlos, John, 236
Carmichael, Stokely, 235, 252
Carnera, Primo, 170
Carson, Benjamin S., *267,* 267–68
Carson, Kit, 72
Carver, George Washington, 81, *95,* 95, *96,*
    96–97
CDF. *See* Children's Defense Fund
Central High School, 209, 273–75
Charbonneau, Toussaint, 37
chemistry, 186–87
Chicago, Illinois, founding of, 18–19
Chicago Defender, 122–23, 127, 132–33, 137,
    179–80
Children's Defense Fund (CDF), 237–38
Church, Robert, 112
churches, importance of, 33
Cinque, Joseph (Sengbe Pieh), *45,* 45–47
Civil Rights Act (1964), 226, 232
civil rights activists and leaders, 109–11,
    112–13, 117–18, 119–21, 122–23, 134–35,
    176–77, 199—201, 204–5, 211–12,
    218–19, 225–26, 229–33, 248–50, 251–52
Civil Rights Movement, 33, 65, 77, 155, 177,
    185, 193, 195, 199–201, 205, 209–10,
    211–12, 213–14, 215–17, 221, 229–33,
    234–36, 240, 248, 251, 257, 270
Civil War, 47, 53, 56, 58, 60, 62, 65, 68–69,
    70, 76, 78
    soldiers, 71, *72,* 72–75, 78, 89
Civilian Conservation Corps, 184
Clark, William, 36–37
Clay, Cassius. *See* Ali, Muhammad
Cleveland, Grover, 101
Coffin, Levi, *52,* 53
Coleman, Elizabeth "Bessie," *136,* 136–37
Colored National Union, 88
Color Purple, The, 258, 264
Coltrane, John, 190, 191, 191
comedian, 253–55

Commoner, The, 93
composer, 91–92, 126–27, 153–54
Confederate States of America, 70
Congo Free State, 94
Congress, U.S., 36, 52, 67, 69, 76, 79, 112, 252
Congressional Medal of Honor, 75, 90, 116
congressmen, 68–69, 79, 251–52
Congress of Racial Equality (CORE),
    216–17, 224, 230, 234
Connor, Eugene "Bull," 216
Continental Congress, 27, 52
Coolidge, Calvin, 118, 139, 166
Cornish, James, 100, 101
Cornwallis, Charles, 28–29
Cosby, Bill, *253*, 253–55
Cotton Club, 154
Covey, Edward, 64
cowboy, 83–84
Craft, Ellen, 58
Craft, William, 58
Crisis, The, 120, 135, *140*, 140, 147

dance, 227–28
Dance Theater of Harlem, 228
Daughters of the American Revolution
    (DAR), 171
Davis, Jefferson, 70
Davis, Miles, 190, 190–91, 202
Days of Grace, 260
Deadwood Dick. *See* Love, Nat
Defender. See Chicago Defender
Dexter Avenue Baptist Church, 200, 229, 230
diplomat, 134–35, 188–89
Dodson, Jacob, 72
Do the Right Thing, 260–70
Douglas, Stephen A., 70
Douglass, Frederick, 52, 53, 56, 61, 63,
    63–65, 67, 73, 93, 103, 112, 146
Drew, Charles Richard, *178*, 178–80
Du Bois, W. E. B., *119*, 119–21, 152
Dunbar High School, 151

Dunn, Oscar J., 79
DuSable, Jean Baptiste Pointe, *18*, 18–19
Dust Tracks on a Road, 145

Eakins, Thomas, 107
"East St. Louis Toodle-Oo," 154
Eckford, Elizabeth, 209, 273–75
Eckstine, Billy, 190
Edelman, Marian Wright, *237*, 237–38
editor, 246–47
educator, 80–82, 95–97, 100–101, 112–13,
    117–18, 119–21, 149–50
Eisenhower, Dwight D., 118, 172, 173
Elder, Lee, 271
Ellington, Edward Kennedy "Duke," *153*,
    153–54
Emancipation Proclamation, The, 70–71, 73,
    224
Emerson, John, 55
Emperor Jones, The, 167
Evans, Gil, 190
Evers, Medgar, 196, *211*, 211–12
Executive Order 8802, 177
Executive Order 9981, 177
Exodusters, 132
explorer, 36–37, 48–49, 114–16

Fairbank, Calvin, 57–58
Fair Employment Practices Committee, 177
Fair Housing Act (1968), 226
Farmer, James, 216, 224
Fifteenth Amendment, 77
Fifty-fourth Massachusetts Regiment, 74
Fire Next Time, The, 194
Fitzgerald, Ella, 143, 160, *161*, 161
Foreman, George, 245
Fort Dade, Treaty of, 41
Fort Gibson, Treaty of, 41
Fort Sumter, 68, 69, 70
Four Little Girls, 270
Fourteenth Amendment, 77

Franklin, Benjamin, 52
Frazier, Joe, 245
Free African Society, 33
Freedmen's Bureau, 76
Freedom Riders, 67, 215–17, 230, 251
Freeman, Elizabeth, *30*, 30–31
Frémont, John, 48–49, 72
French and Indian War, 17
frontiersman, 18–19, 48–49
Fugitive Slave Law, 53

Gaines, Lloyd Lionel, 206, 207
Gandhi, Mahatma, 229, 251, 252
Garrison, William Lloyd, 52, 67
Garvey, Marcus, *138*, 138–39, 220
Get on the Bus, 270
Gibson, Althea, 259
Gillespie, Dizzy, 190
golf, 271–72
Goodman, Robert, 249
Go Tell It on the Mountain, 195
Graham, Henry, 217
Grant, Ulysses S., 76
Granz, Norman, 161
Great Depression, 131, 133, 141, 154, 163, 184
Great Gabriel Conspiracy, 34
Great Northern Migration, The, 113, 122, 132–33
Grey, Samuel, 21

Haley, Alex Palmer, *202*, 202–3
Hamer, Fannie Lou, *218*, 218–19
Handy, William Christopher, *126*, 126–27
Hansberry, Lorraine, *192*, 192–93
Hard Road to Glory, A, 260
Harlem, 139, 154, 161, 170, 204, 228
Harlem Renaissance, 140–41, 144, 147
Harlem Suitcase Theatre, 148
Harpers Ferry, 146
Harpo Productions, 264

Hayden, Lewis, *57*, 57–58
Hayes, Rutherford B., 77
Head Start, 237–38
heart operation, 100–101
He Got Game, 270
Hellfighter, 129
Henson, Matthew Alexander, *114*, 114–16
Higginson, Thomas Wentworth, 58
historian, 93–94, 151–52
History of the African-American Athlete, A, 260
History of the Negro Race in America from 1619 to 1880, 94
Hitler, Adolf, 157, 170
Holiday, Billie, 131, *160*, 160–61
Horse, John, 41–42
Houston, Charles Hamilton, *155*, 155–56
Howard University, 144, 149, 150, 155, 156, 186, 188, 206, 247, 256
Hughes, Langston, *146*, 146–48, 193
humanitarian. *See* philanthropy
Hurston, Zora Neale, *144*, 144–45, 152, 258

I Spy, 253

Jack, Gullah, 38
Jackson, Jesse, *248*, 248–50
Jackson, Jimmy Lee, 232
Jackson, Mahalia, 131
"Jamaica Train," 50
jazz music, 142–43, 160–61, 190–91
Jefferson, Thomas, 23, 36
Jemison, Mae C., 241, *243*, 243
Jesup, Thomas Sidney, 40
Jim Crow laws, 77
Johnson, Henry, *128*, 128–29
Johnson, James P., 131
Johnson, James Weldon, 120, *134*, 134–35
Johnson, Lyndon, 208, 214, 219, 232, 236
Johnson, Marguerite. *See* Angelou, Maya
Jones, Absalom, 32–33
Joplin, Scott, *91*, 91–92

Jordan, George, 89–90
Jordan, Michael Jeffrey, *265*, 265–66
Journal of Negro History, 152
journalism, 109–11
Julian, Percy Lavon, 186, 186–87, 188
Just Give Me a Cool Drink of Water 'fore I Diiie, 240

Kaffir Boy, 264
Kennedy, John F., 173, 212, 224, 231, 251
Kennedy, Robert, 217, 238, 252
King, Coretta Scott, 230, 254
King, Martin Luther, Jr., 200, 201, 217, 224, 228, *229*, 229–33, 235, 248, 252
Ku Klux Klan, 77, 130, 132, 200, 205, 217, 220

labor leader, 87–88, 176–77
Lafayette, Marquis de, 28–29, 52
Lake Okeechobee, Battle of, 42
Langston, Mary, 146–47
law profession, 93–94, 155–56, 206–8
Learning Tree, The, 185
Leary, Lewis Sheridan, 146
Lee, Bill, 269
Lee, George T., 211
Lee, Robert E., 76
Lee, Shelton Jackson "Spike," *269*, 269–70
"Letter from Birmingham City Jail," 231
Lewis, John Robert, *251*, 251–52
Lewis, Meriwether, 36–37
Lincoln, Abraham, 65, 67, 70, *71*, 71, 72, 73, 74
Lindsay, Vachel, 147
Little, Malcolm. *See* Malcolm X
Little Rock Nine, The, *209*, 209–10
Locke, Alain Leroy, 144, *149*, 149–50
Loguen, Jermain Wesley, 53, *61*, 61–62
Louis, Joe, *169*, 169–70, 182
Louisiana Purchase, 36–37
Love, Nat, *83*, 83–84

Lovejoy, Elijah, 53
Love Supreme, A, 191
lynchings, 65, 69, 109—11, 112, 135, 161, 251

Malcolm X, 202, *220*, 220–22, 235, 270
"Man Who Lived Underground, The," 164
"Maple Leaf Rag," 92
March on Washington, The (1963), 177, 223–24, 226, 251
Marshall, Thurgood, 156, *206*, 206–8, 210
mathematics, 22–23
Matzeliger, Jan Ernst, 85, 85–86
McCain, Franklin, *213*, 213
McCoy, Elijah, *106*, 106
McKissick, Floyd, 224
McNeil, Joseph, *213*, 213
"Memphis Blues," 126
Meridian, 258
Metcalfe, Ralph, 159
Mexican War, 251
Micanopy (Seminole chief), 41
migration to North, 113, 122, 132–33
military, 26–27, 71, *72*, 72–75, 78, 89–90, 93, 104–5, 128–29, 133, 134, 177, 255–56
Miller, G. P., 72
Million Man March, 270
minister, 61–62, 248–50
Mississippi Freedom Democratic Party (MFDP), 205, 219
Missouri Compromise, 56
Mitchell, Arthur, 227, *228*, 228
Monk, Thelonious, 191
Montés, 45
Montgomery Improvement Association (MIA), 200
Montgomery, Hugh, 21
"Mood Indigo," 154
Morgan, Garrett Augustus, 124–25
Morrison, Toni, *246*, 246–47, 264
movies, 184–85, 258, 264, 269–70
Muhammad, Elijah, 221

music, 91–92, 130–31, 126–27, 142–43,
    153–54, 160–61, 167–68, 171–73, 190–91
mutinies on slave ship, 45–47
Myers, Isaac, 87–88

Narrative of the Life of Frederick Douglass,
    An American Slave, 64
National Aeronautics and Space
    Administration (NASA), 242, 243
National Association for the Advancement of
    Colored People (NAACP), 103, 111, 113,
    119, 120, 123, 134, 135, 140, 156, 192,
    199, 200, 204, 206, 208, 210, 211, 224,
    225, 226, 234, 237
National Association of Colored Women
    (NACW), 113
National Baseball League, 261
National Book Award, 203, 258
National Council of Negro Women, 118
National Negro Business League, 81
National Urban League, 140
National Youth Administration (NYA), 118
Nation of Islam, 221–22, 235, 244
Native Americans, 16–17, 18, 37, 40–42,
    48–49, 89
Native Son, 164, 264
Negro American Labor Council, 177
Negro Baseball League, 174–75, 181
Negro Factories Corporation, 139
Nemiroff, Robert, 193
New Deal, 123
New Negro, The, 144, 150
newspapers
    Chicago Defender, 122–23, 127, 132–33,
        137, 179–80
    Cleveland Call, 125
    Colored Citizen, 88
    Daily American, 134
    Free Speech, 110
    Headlight, 110
    Kansas City *Call,* 226

    Living Way, 109
    Muhammad Speaks, 221
    Negro World, 139
    New Orleans Lousianian, 79
    North Star, 61, 65
    St. Paul *Appeal,* 226
New York Age, 111
Niagara Movement, 120
1963 March on Washington, The, 177,
    223–24, 226, 251
Ninth Cavalry, 89–90
Ninth Ohio Volunteer Cavalry, 104
Nixon, Edgar Daniel, 200
Nixon, Richard, 255
Nobel Peace Prize, 188, 189, 232
Nobel Prize for Literature, 247
North Pole exploration, 114–16
Not Without Laughter, 148
Nuremberg Laws, 118

O'Brien, W. J., 187
Off the Court, 260
Officers' Candidate School (OCS), 182
Oliver, Joe "King," 142–43
"Ol' Man River," 168
Olustee, Battle of, 74
Olympic Games, 157–59, 197—98, 244, 245,
    265, 266
Once, 257
O'Neill, Eugene, 167
opera singer, 171–73
Operation Breadbasket, 232, 248, 249
orator, 63–65
Organization of Afro-American Unity
    (OAAU), 221
Osceola (chief), 41–42
Othello, 168
Owens, Jesse, 157, 157, 158, 158–59

Pace, Henry, 127
Paige, Leroy Robert "Satchel," *174,* 174–75, 270

Paine, Thomas, 25, 52
Palmer, Henry, 100
Parker, Charlie, 190
Parks, Gordon, *184*, 184–85
Parks, Rosa, *199*, 199–201, 229, 230, 251
patriot, 20–21
Peace Corps, 243, 252
peanuts, study of, 95–97
Peary, Robert E., 114–16
pediatric neurosurgeon, 267–68
People United to Serve Humanity (PUSH),
    249
Pershing, John J., 105
Persian Gulf War, 256
Peters, John, 25
philanthropy, 103, 255
philosophy, 149–50
photography, 184–85
physician, 178–80
pilot, 136–37
Pinchback, P. B. S., *78*, 78–79
Pinkerton, Allen, 52
Pitcairn, John, 26
plaintiff in slave lawsuit, 55–56
Planter, 68, 69
Plessy v. Ferguson, 206, 207
Poem on Various Subjects, Religious and Moral,
    24
poetry, 16–17, 24–25, 146–48, 239–40
political activist, 167–68
Poor People's Campaign, 238
Possessing the Secret of Joy, 258
postal stamp honors, 60, 137
Powell, Colin Luther, *255*, 255–56
Poyas, Peter, 38, 39
preacher, 32–33, 66–67
presidential advisor, 80–82
Presidential Medal of Freedom, 159, 238, 256
Prince, Lucy Terry, 16–17
Prosser, Gabriel, 34–35
Pulitzer Prize, 203, 240, 247, 258

ragtime, 91–92
Rainbow Coalition, 250
Rainey, Gertrude "Ma," 130
Raisin in the Sun, A, 192, 193
Randolph, Asa Philip, *176*, 176–77, 223
Ray, James Earl, 233
Reconstruction, 76–77, 78–79
Red Cross, 179
Reeb, James, 232
religious leader. *See* minister; preacher
Relyea, Captain, 68, 69
Revolutionary Petunias & Other Poems, 258
Revolutionary War, 26–27, 28–29
Richmond, David, *213*, 213
Rickey, Branch, 182
Rillieux, Norbert, 50
Roberts, Needham, 128–29
Robeson, Paul, *167*, 167–68
Robinson, Jackie, *181*, 181–83, 261
Roosevelt, Eleanor, 171
Roosevelt, Franklin, 118, 123, 177
Roosevelt, Theodore, 81, 118, 134
Roots, 202–3
Rosamond, John, 134
Rudolph, Wilma, *197*, 197—98
Ruggles, David, 64
Rustin, Bayard, 223–24
Ruth, Babe, 261, 262

Sacajawea, 37
Sadat, Anwar, 248
sailor, 20–21
Salem, Peter, *26*, 26–27
Schmeling, Max, 170
school desegregation, 145, 207–8, 209–10,
    273–75
schools for African-Americans, 61, 76,
    117–18
science, 95–97, 178–80
Scott, Dred, *55*, 55–56
scout, 36–37, 48–49, 60

Sedgwick, Theodore, 30–31
Selma March, 248
Seminole Wars, 40–42
Semple, Jesse B., 148
Sengbe Pieh. *See* Cinque, Joseph
Shaft, 185
sharecropping, defining, 218
Shaw, Artie, 160
Shepard, Alan B., 242
She's Gotta Have It, 269
ship-caulking business, 87
shoe manufacturing, 85–86
Showboat, 168
Simple Stories, The, 148
Sinclair, Patrick, 19
singers, 130–31, 160–61, 167–68, 171–73
sit-ins, 195, 205, 213–14, 223, 226, 230, 235, 237, 248, 251
Sixteenth Street Baptist Church, 270
slave rebellions, 34–35, 38–39, 43–44, 45–47
Smalls, Robert, *68*, 68–69
Smith, Bessie, *130*, 130–31, 160
Smith, Tommie, *235*, 236
Smith, Willie "the Lion," 154
soldiers. *See* military
"Solitude," 154
Song of Solomon, 247
"Sophisticated Lady," 154
Souls of Black Folk, The, 120
Southern Christian Leadership Conference (SCLC), 205, 219, 230, 232, 234, 248, 249
soybeans, research on, 96, 186–87
Spanish-American War, 90, 101, 104
Spinks, Leon, 245
sports, 157–59, 167, 169–70, 174–75, 181–83, 197–98, 244–45, 259–60, 261–62, 265–66, 271–72
spy, 28–29, 60
Stand for Children, 238
state legislator, 57–58
Stevens, Thaddeus, 52, 77

Stewart, Eliza, 78
"St. Louis Blues," 127
Stowe, Harriet Beecher, 52, 53
Stride Toward Freedom, 230
Student Nonviolent Coordinating Committee (SNCC), 205, 217, 219, 224, 230, 232, 235, 251
Sula, 247
Sumner, Charles, 77
Supreme Court, U.S., 46, 55, 56, 145, 156, 168, 192, 200, 201, 206, 207, 208, 210, 245
surgeon, 100–101
Survey Graphic, 149–50
surveyor, 22–23
Sweatt, Herman, 207
Sweatt v. Painter, 207

Taft, William Howard, 81
"Take the A Train," 154
Taney, Roger B., 56
Tanner, Henry Ossawa, *107*, 107–8
Tar Baby, 247
Taylor, Tom, 75
Taylor, Zachary, 42
television, 203, 231, 233, 253–54, 263–64
Temple, Lewis, 54
Temple of My Familiar, 258
tennis, 259–60
Tenth Cavalry, 89–90
Terrell, Mary Church, 112, 112–13
Terry, Lucy. *See* Prince, Lucy Terry
Their Eyes Were Watching God, 145, 258
Third Life of Grange Copeland, The, 258
Thirteenth Amendment, 62, 77
Thoreau, Henry David, 52, 251
Till, Emmett, 196, 251
To Be Young, Gifted, and Black, 193
toggle, *54*, 54
track and field, 157–59, 197–98
Travis, Joseph, 43

Treemonisha, 92
Truman, Harry, 118, 177
Trumbauer, Horace, 165, 166
Truth, Sojourner, 52, *66*, 66–67
Tubman, Harriet Ross, 52, 53, 59, 59–60, 146
Turner, Nat, *43*, 43–44
Tuskegee Institute, 80–82, 96, 97, 103, 138

Uncle Tom's Children, 163
Underground Railroad, The, 51–53, 54, 58, 59–60, 61–62, 106
Union Army, 58, 60, 72–75, 78
Union Baptist Church, 94
union organizer. *See* labor leader
United Nations (UN), 189
United Negro College Fund, 256
Universal Negro Improvement Association (UNIA), 138–39
University of California, Los Angeles (UCLA), 181, 259
Up from Slavery, 81

Van Buren, Martin, 46
Vesey, Denmark, *38*, 38–39
Vietnam War, 241, 244–45, 255
voting rights, 77, 199
    voter registration, 205, 211–12, 218–19, 234, 249, 257
    women's, 113
Voting Rights Act (1965), 226, 232

Walker, Alice, *257*, 257–58, 264
Walker, Madam C. J., 102–3
Waller, Fats, 154
Walsh, Molly, 22
Washington, Booker T., *80*, 80–82, 96, 120, 138, 139
Washington, George, 25, 27, 28
Washington Research Project, 238
Washingtonians, the, 154

Watts riot, 235–36
Ways of White Folks, The, 148
Weary Blues, The, 148
Webb, William "Chick," 161
Webster, Delia, 57
Wells-Barnett, Ida B., *109*, 109–11, 112
West Point, 104, 105
whaling industry, 54
Wheatley, Phillis, *24*, 24–25
White, William, 32
White Citizens council, 200
Whittier, John Greenleaf, 52
Wild Cat, 42
Wilkins, Roy, 224, *225*, 225–26
Williams, Daniel Hale, *100*, 100–101
Williams, George Washington, *93*, 93–94
Williams, Paul Revere, 165, *166*, 166
Wilson, Woodrow, 129, 134–35
Winfrey, Oprah, 258, *263*, 263–64
Wofford, Chloe Anthony. *See* Morrison, Toni
Women of Brewster Place, 264
women's rights, 58, 60, 64, 65, 66–67, 113, 118, 204
Women Wage-Earners Association, 113
Woods, Granville T., *98*, 98–99
Woods, Tiger, *271*, 271–72
Woodson, Carter G., *151*, 151–52
World View of Race, A, 189
World War I, 113, 122, 125, 127, 128–29, 132–33, 136, 140, 177
World War II, 133, 154, 170, 175, 177, 178, 182, 184, 187, 189, 202
Wright, Richard, *162*, 162–64, 195
writers, 134–35, 144–45, 146–48, 149–50, 162–64, 184–85, 192–93, 194–96, 202–3, 239–40, 246–47, 253–55, 257–58

York, *36*, 36–37
Yorktown, Battle of, 29
Young, Charles, *104*, 104–5
Young Negroes Cooperative League, 204

Photo Credits

About the Author

Susan Altman's publications include *The Encyclopedia of African-American Heritage, Followers of the North Star,* and the play *Out of the Whirlwind.* She is co-author of the Modern Rhymes About Ancient Times series (Children's Press 2001). Altman produces the Emmy Award-winning *It's Academic,* television's longest-running high school quiz show. She has also produced *Pick Up the Beat,* a popular TV show that explores topics of interest to teenagers, and two Emmy-winning children's programs: *It's Elementary* and *Head's Up!* Altman lives in Washington, D.C.